Narcissistic Abuse

A Guide To Narcissistic Abuse Syndrome Survival

By

Damon Colmain

The trademarks that are used are without any consent, and the publication of the trademark is without permission or backing by the trademark owner. All trademarks and brands within this book are for clarifying purposes only and are owned by the owners themselves, not affiliated with this document.

Table of contents

Chapter 1: Introduction

The topic 'Narcissism' has interested us for a long time, yet social researchers currently guarantee that it has become a "modern epidemic." The term narcissism was coined by Paul Nacke in 1899 to portray somebody who treated their own body as though it were a sexual article, instead of having sexual wants for others. Dr. Freud Sigmund paper 'On Narcissism.' He advanced this new idea through his work on the 'self-image' and its connection to the outer world.
Narcissism can be characterized as the quest for gratification from egotistic or vanity admiration of one's attributes.

Narcissism lies on a continuum from beneficial to obsessive. Healthy narcissism is a piece of ordinary human functioning. It speaks to required self - love and certainty dependent on genuine accomplishments and the capacity to overcome setbacks. But, narcissism turns into an issue when one turns out to be excessively engrossed with oneself and seeks complete admiration and attention, with a complete dismissal of others' feelings. Lack of satisfaction of this need prompts substance misuse and major depressive disorders. In teenagers, this causes 'Substance Dependency Disorder' (SDD) - they show plain narcissism, which offers an association between self-centeredness and fixation. These substances incorporate tranquilizers like liquor, and psychedelic drugs like LSD, energizers like cocaine, opiates like opium, heroin, morphine, and against nervousness drugs like Xanax.

Kurt Cobain says, "I couldn't care less what you think, except if it is about me." This demonstrates the narcissist's lack of interest for others except if it explicitly identifies with them. They are incapable of a genuine interest in others except if they are required for the previous' statement of prevalence. Narcissists are extraordinary con -artist; all things considered, they generally prevail with regards to seducing themselves. It turns out to be incredibly agonizing when they experience memory misfortune when they miss out on pieces of the individual they love the most. A narcissist "eats up individuals, devours their yield, and throws the void, wreathing shells aside," says Sam Vaknin. Despise is a supplement of dread, and the narcissists like being dreaded - it gives them an inebriating vibe of supremacy. The contrast between Narcissism and self - love involves profundity. Narcissus begins to look all starry eyed not with oneself, yet with a picture or impression of oneself, with the persona, the cover. Narcissists see themselves through others' eyes, change their way of life, and conduct and articulate sentiments, as per others' profound respect. Narcissism is a deliberate visual deficiency, a deal to avoid looking underneath the surface.

Todd Solondz says, "Narcissism and self-misdirection are survival components without which a considerable lot of us may just jump off the bridge." For genuine narcissists, the resistances are critical to repay their personality shortfalls and lessen disgrace feelings.

According to TS Eliot, "... a large portion of the mischief is done in the world right now because of individuals who need to feel significant. They don't intend to do hurt, yet the mischief [that they cause] doesn't intrigue them. Or then again, they don't see it, or they legitimize it since they are caught up in the eternal battle to have a favorable opinion of themselves." This shows differentiation between malignant narcissists and the individuals who need to worry about how their conduct may antagonistically influence others. It is yet another method for picking up thoughtfulness regarding their supreme self -absorption, which makes it outlandish for them to relate to others' feelings.

Narcissism is characterized as "over the top interest with oneself; self-love; vanity" or in psychoanalytic terms as "sensual delight derived from the reverence of one's own physical or mental qualities, being a typical condition at the juvenile level of character development." This term is utilized for basic self-assimilation. In 1968, an outrageous structure was added to the psychological literature as a quantifiable finding.

Statistics show the increase in Narcissism levels in recent decades, among the school-going understudies, for example, the young; they are seen as wild creatures for the general public in the USA. These adolescents are the future chiefs, and Narcissism is exceptionally hurtful to the general public overall. It can cause disappointment in academic and different undertakings. Twenge and Campbell led a review in American foundations from 1979 - 2006. They found an upward move in scores on the NPI, implying that, presently, the typical average college student grasps narcissistic propensities more than their partners, two decades prior. The rise in Narcissism in the American population maybe because now, since early on, Americans are encouraged that they are exceptional and one of a kind, which expands their self-awareness. Extroversion and declaration are the critical variables of Narcissism. It is also because of the enormous emphasis on materialism and riches, focusing on a person's pleasure and achievement in the present American culture.

Today, Narcissism has grasped the whole world, as demonstrated by the public's fast change during industrial and post-modern occasions. The previous decades have seen a cultural move about the group to attention on the individual or self. Here comes in 'oneself - regard development,' which turned into achievement throughout everyday life. The guardians attempted to "present" self-in regarding their kids instead of permitting them to accomplish it through challenging work. The ascent of independence and the decrease in social standards that went with society's modernization prompted a move from the idea of what is best for the others and family to what is best for "me." With an all-out spotlight on riches and fame, the business world made a "vacant self, shorn of social importance." Today, the age of youthful grown-ups - the 'Generation Y' - otherwise called the 'Millennial' and 'Generation Me,' containing people conceived between 1975 - 1995, is condemned for being narcissistic, narrow-minded, self - entitled, and having ridiculous desires from life. The current Diagnostic and Statistical Manual (DSM-V) of the American Psychiatric Association characterizes Narcissistic Personality Disorder as an example of pretentiousness. The requirement for appreciation and absence of sympathy is starting by early adulthood. The 'American Psychiatry Association' has grouped this as 'Narcissistic Personality Disorder' (NPD).

THE ORIGIN

The term 'narcissism' began from the Roman artist Ovid's Metamorphoses (Book III) in Narcissus and Echo's primary century story, many centuries later advanced into a profoundly specific psychoanalytic term. In Ovid's legend, Narcissus is an attractive youngster who spurns the advances of numerous potential lovers, including the sprite Echo, named this way because she was cursed only to echo the sounds that others made. After Narcissus rejects Echo, the god beings to punish him by making him hopelessly enamored with his appearance in a pool, finding that the object of his adoration can't cherish him back; he dies. Narcissism has a complex and rich history in clinical analysis writing, starting with a solid spotlight on unusual self-centered sexuality. The principal therapist who utilized the expression "Narcissus-like" clinically was Havelock Ellis (1898), who connected Ovid's legend to the state of "auto-suggestion" (for example, self as claim sexual article) in one of his patients.

Freud (1905/1953) correspondingly first utilized the expressions "ego" (self-love) and "narcissistic charisma" reciprocally in his 3 Essays on the Concept of Sexuality. Freud's and Ellis' psychoanalytic narcissism both encompassed an immature, solely self-satisfying sexuality that isn't a piece of its clinical definition today. A couple of years later, the idea of selfishness started to incorporate certain two qualities increasingly well-known to the character and social clinicians today. As far as anyone is concerned, Ernest Jones (1913/1951) was the first to translate narcissism as a character attribute he called the "God-complex." He described individuals with the God-complex as aloof, unavailable, self-appreciating, vainglorious, presumptuous, auto-sexual, and exhibitionistic, with dreams of power and omniscience. He additionally saw that these individuals had a strict requirement for uniqueness ("… nothing irritates such a man as the proposal that he takes after another person… " p. 252) and acclaim from others. This description is astoundingly near the present origination of Narcissistic Personality Disorder, portrayed in the following area. At almost a similar time, Freud (1914/1991) distributed his introductory essay On Narcissism: An Introduction, composing from an increasingly formative perspective. To him, narcissism was an ordinary maturational period of substantial improvement in all youngsters, a "supplement to the selfishness of nature for self-conservation."

Freud hypothesized that before children can contribute their "libidinal" vitality in others, they experience a versatile time of essential narcissism. They are egocentric and can't take others' points of view. Healthy development " consists of a departure from primary narcissism " when individuals put their libidinal energy into someone else as opposed to themselves. Freud trusted in an economic model of affection in which every one of us has restricted intense energy that can only be invested in one place at a time. In this manner, when individuals progress from essential narcissism to object love, their feeling of self-respect are brought down. A healthy relationship is proportional, with the two individuals putting their libidinal energy into one another, and neither encountering a misfortune, therefore.

Nonetheless, when individuals love objects can't or reluctant to restore the adoration, they three relapses to an undesirable condition of narcissism, called secondary narcissism, to cherish and delight themselves as compensatory mechanisms. Wälder (1925) published the primary contextual investigation of somebody with a confused narcissistic personality. His patient was a researcher with an attitude of superiority, failure to relate to other people, a feeling of being "not quite the same as humankind as a rule," a fixation on cultivating a sense of pride, an absence of common sentiments of blame, infantile sexuality, and a stamped freedom from others.

Wälder's patient was likewise excessively consistent and expository and esteemed unique intellectual ideas (thinking for the good of thinking) over the use of logical information to human development. Wälder's contextual analysis was compelling in the manner we characterize narcissism as a personality disorder today. Freud took action accordingly in portraying the narcissistic personality in his 1931 exposition, Libidinal Types. He described a narcissist as somebody centered around self-preservation, autonomous, not effortlessly scared, forceful, extraverted, high in movement, and incapable of adoring or committing in a relationship. He likewise noticed that these individuals regularly draw in a great deal of adoration and consideration and promptly take on influential positions. Presently psychoanalyst Wilhelm Reich (1933) portrayed a "phallic-narcissistic character" in his book Character Analysis. According to him, narcissists have an attitude of superiority, are confident, arrogant, provocative, resent subordination, and are mildly sadistic in their relationships. Reich additionally was the first to take note that if narcissists were ego-threatened, they would get forceful: "If their vanity is offended, they respond with cold hatred, stamped bad mood, or absolute hostility."

Reich's perspective on narcissism is, to some degree, weaved with masculinity by four definitions. He considers it an "identification between the inner self overall and the phallus," and he conjectures that this issue is more typical in men than in ladies.

Karen Horney (1939) further built up the possibility of narcissism as a character quality, concentrating for the most part on more unmistakably characterizing the many "dissimilar" representations of selfishness. She likewise hypothesized its causes and results. Horney described narcissism as just "self-expansion," implying that the narcissist "cherishes and respects himself for values for which there is no satisfactory establishment." She didn't think it was selfish to value qualities one had, and indeed, to her, this was the meaning of genuine self-esteem.

Horney concurred with Freud's thought that secondary narcissism comes from an absence of affection from guardians. She thought this went through in either excessive dictator or tolerant child parenting styles. She felt that if guardians didn't adore kids for their 'genuine selves,' kids would react by making fanciful expanded adaptations of themselves. They would look for esteem and consideration as pay. However, Horney couldn't help contradicting Freud's thought that narcissists can't adore others since they love themselves to an extreme. Instead, she sees the outward showcase of self-esteem to be fanciful and accepts that narcissism originates from powerlessness to cherish one's actual self or any other person. Horney saw desperate outcomes in both the careers and love lives of narcissists if kids' "narcissistic pattern" was not outgrown. In their professions, narcissists have a shallow and inefficient working style joined with expanding privilege or the "desire that commitment or greatness can be achieved without exertion and activity."

Narcissists likewise will, in general, look for shallow relationships that add to their status and renown, have exclusive standards of others, poor social skills (for example, conceit, hostility, doubt, lack of engagement in others), and exceptionally unreasonable perspectives on themselves. This places them in the genuinely vulnerable situation of requiring individuals to appreciate and support them, however experiencing issues finding individuals who will keep on doing this. In this manner, Horney's narcissists are consistently in a condition of distance from oneself and other people.

Annie Reich (1960) portrayed narcissists as "individuals whose charisma is, for the most part, concentrated on them at the detriment of object love" and who have "misrepresented, unreasonable – i.e., puerile – internal measuring sticks." Reich accepted that narcissism is brought about by rehashed youth injuries that happen before the inner self's guard systems are created and lead the youngster to withdraw internally to a more secure self-defensive dreamland: "It isn't so. I am not defenseless, dying, demolished. Despite what might be expected, I am greater and better than any other individual. I am the greatest, the most glorious. Reich likewise guessed that narcissists experience the ill effects of a failure to control their confidence. They are moving drastically from the statures of self-importance to the profundities of melancholy. In the principal period of the cycle, narcissists participate in moderately minor activities and attach inflated importance to them that others don't share. As such, narcissists become cheerful and "self-beguiled" until they experience some sort 6 of rude awakening (for example, a disappointment, primary input). This makes them respond unexpectedly with outrageous depression, which Reich thinks comes from their high contrast narrow mindedness of vagueness. They may consider themselves great or an all-out disappointment, with hardly any degrees in the middle. When feeling despair, they will search out others with whom they can glorify and recognize and relax in these others' shine.

Narcissists' assessments of others additionally significantly move in cycles since others are utilized as devices to develop their self-images. Inglorious times, others are viewed as descending correlation targets; however, others are viewed as persuasive upward examination targets on desperate occasions. Kohut (1966, 1968, 1971, 1972) composed widely on narcissism, and like Freud, he also accepted that narcissism was a solid and typical piece of advancement and "neither obsessive nor unsavory" (1966). However, in contrast to Freud, he accepted that essential narcissism was a condition of undifferentiated association with the mother, as opposed to a state of complete self-retention: " the baby originally experiences the mother and her ministrations not as you and its activities, yet inside a perspective on the world where the separation has not yet been built up." From this state, he set two separate formative directions of a spotlight on self and others, which also diverges from Freud's monetary libidinal model. As adoration increments for the other, it relatively diminishes for oneself.

Instead, Kohut felt that these different directions could work autonomously of one another all through life expectancy. The other tangible advancements or horrible interferences that could happen would prompt distinctive grown-up character groups of stars. A healthy developmental sequence of the idealized parent occurs with a continuous acknowledgment of one's guardians' uncertainty. This acknowledgment prompts the disguise of a solid superego and, with it, a feeling of beliefs that we can endeavor to reach for the duration of our lives.

The healthy developmental sequence of the grandiose self includes the steady presentation to and acknowledgment of one's frailty through the guardians' caring help. In development, the solid pretentious self can be shown from a healthy perspective of funniness, sagacity, uniqueness, aspirations, confidence, and a: "sound delight in our exercises and victories and ... a valuable adaptive feeling of dissatisfaction tinged with outrage and disgrace over our eight failures and shortcomings" (Kohut, 1966).

Kohut was amazingly condemning religion and other cultural establishments that attempted to stifle the versatile articulation of narcissism (i.e., self-esteem); he felt that a definite self-esteem feeling is essential to sound mental working. Nonetheless, Kohut believed that there could be undesirable articulations of the bombastic self that could create when people neglected to coordinate pompous thoughts with reasonable perspectives on their disappointments and deficiencies. He felt this was brought about by a horrible interference of the sound narcissistic improvement through parental "dismissal and overindulgence" (Kohut, 1966) and that if the vainglorious self-had not developed into a practical feeling of self-esteem, "then the grown-up personality will, in general, waver between an unreasonable overestimation of oneself and sentiments of inadequacy and will respond with narcissistic humiliation to the upsetting of its aspirations" (Kohut, 1966).

Subsequently, narcissists would use a lot of vitality in looking for confirmation from individuals and being excessively powerless against analysis and dismissal. Kohut prescribed that treatment for undesirable narcissism ought to include a procedure of reflecting where the advisor initially attests their feeling of pretentiousness at that point guides them tenderly and steadily toward an acknowledgment of their restrictions and practical self-esteem. It is prominent that Kohut additionally established the framework for a hypothesis of narcissistic hostility after a sense of self-risk that has gotten practical help as of late (for example, Bushman and Baumeister, 1998) by proposing that "narcissistic anger" would happen because of seeing wounds to the inner self (Kohut, 1972). Otto Kernberg also composed widely on narcissistic scatters, accepting that they were a subtype of marginal character issues (Kernberg, 1975).

NARCISSISTIC PATHOLOGY AND BEHAVIOR

Research discoveries utilizing the NPI portray a picture of narcissists as having expanded and pompous mental self-views. It isn't astounding then that narcissists report having high confidence. But, this positive mental self-views has all the earmarks of being founded on the wrong and expanded impression of their achievements and their contorted perspectives on others' opinion of them. For instance, they overestimate their physical attractiveness relative to judges' evaluations of their engaging quality, and they overestimate their insight relative to objective assessments of their IQ. In one test, narcissistic and no narcissistic men (as distinguished based on their NPI results) were met by a lady whose reactions were scripted; thus, all the men got a similar social criticism. In any case, the narcissistic men surveyed the lady's appreciation for them more profoundly than did no narcissistic men. Different discoveries show that narcissists assume more noteworthy acknowledgment for good results in any event, whenever those results happened by karma or possibility.

Although narcissists' confidence is high, it is likewise delicate and uncertain, as confirm by its fluctuation. It varies from minute to minute, every day, more than that of less-narcissistic individuals. Other research demonstrates that narcissists are bound to have high unequivocal (cognizant, self-detailed) confidence and low verifiable (nonconscious or automatic) confidence. This finding recommends that although narcissists depict themselves positively, their nonconscious feelings about themselves are not all that positive.

Narcissists' sure, however, unreliable self-view leads them to be increasingly mindful and receptive to criticism from others. In any case, an extraordinary reaction or criticism from others is imperative to narcissists; they are anxious to discover that others respect and admire them. Narcissists value appreciation and predominance more than being enjoyed and acknowledged. Studies find that narcissists' confidence relies on the degree to which they feel appreciated. Besides, narcissists seek profound respect from others by endeavoring to control the impressions they make in others. They make self-advancing and cocky articulations and attempt to request respect and praise from everyone around them. They additionally react with outrage and hatred when they feel compromised by others. They are bound to respond forcefully to such events and disparage the individuals who undermine them, in any event, when such threatening reacting endangers the relationship.

When Narcissistic Behavior Becomes Narcissistic Personality Disorder

In Greek mythology, Narcissus was renowned for his excellence and was glad to such an extent that he hated the individuals who cherished him. Instead, he experienced passionate feelings for his appearance in a pool of water and couldn't leave the picture of himself. At long last, he died, incapable of tearing himself away. His obsession with himself was his demise.

We've all seen narcissistic behavior. The person who overdresses his muscles at the gym, the young lady who goes hours complaining about her hair before the mirror. Typically these individuals are youthful, and their behavior is generally harmless. As their intellectual aptitudes create, they start to comprehend the significance of healthy relationships with others. In the end, they grow up and shed their narcissistic ways.

But, for the individuals who don't develop psychologically, their narcissistic behavior becomes serious. They create Narcissistic Personality Disorder. Unexpectedly, these individuals don't generally cherish themselves; they are simply experts at veiling their low confidence. What's more, similar to Narcissus, they are in danger of being so self-retained as to be a danger to themselves as well as other people. Sadly, they regularly neglect to look for help.

Chapter 2: What Is Narcissistic Personality Disorder (NPD)?

Narcissistic personality disorder (NPD) is one group of cluster B disorders that includes antisocial, histrionic, and borderline. NPD consists of three components: an expanded perspective on oneself, an absence of warmth or compassion in a relationship, and the use of an assortment of techniques for keeping up the inflated self-view. The inflated self-perspectives of those with NPD can incorporate the general feeling of uncommonness, uniqueness, confidence, and privilege combined with specifically inflated self-beliefs (e.g., Campbell, Bonacci, Shelton, Exline, and Bushman, 2004; Emmons, 1984). For instance, there might be the conviction that one is more intelligent, increasingly attractive, or more creative than others. These inflated perspectives will, in general, fall in the area of social dominance instead of social warmth.

Narcissism isn't related to considering oneself to be more mindful and kind than others (Campbell, Rudich, and Sedikides, 2002). Instead, they need to be viewed as beings with high status and capability. Consistent with the view that narcissists are less worried about warmth and closeness than with other admirable attributes, they exhibit a relative lack of engagement in mindful and selflessness in romantic relationships (e.g., Campbell, Foster, and Finkel, 2002). They score low on self-report measures of agreeableness (Bradlee and Emmons, 1992) and projective intimacy measures, for example, the TAT (Carroll, 1987). The absence of warmth, nonetheless, doesn't imply that those with NPD are not social. Quite the contrary, narcissism is associated with social extraversion (Bradlee and Emmons, 1992). More narcissistic people tend to be popular in beginning social gatherings (Paulhus, 1998).

Narcissism is related to the use of a broad scope of techniques for keeping up inflated self-views. These strategies can be categorized as either psychic or relational. Psychically, narcissism is related to fantasies of success and power (Raskin and Novacek, 1991) just as oneself serving inclination (that is, taking credit for success but blaming the situation for failure) (e.g., Campbell, Reeder, Sedikides, and Elliot, 2000). Interpersonally, narcissism is associated with the use of social circumstances for enhancing status and esteem. Such strategies incorporate gloating and bragging (Buss and Chiodo, 1991), contending (Raskin and Terry, 1988), and endeavoring (frequently effectively to exceed expectations at testing assignments when others are watching (Wallace and Baumeister, 2002).

Narcissism is likewise associated with indirect strategies for gaining status and esteem, such as acquiring "trophy" romantic partners (Campbell, 1999) and expensive material products (Vohs and Campbell, 2004). At the point when confronted with the threatening information about oneself, for example, negative input, narcissism can be connected to savagery or hostility against the individuals who Campbell, W. K., and Baumeister, R. F. (2006). Narcissistic personality disorder In J. E. Fisher and W. T. O'Donohue (Eds.), Practitioner's manual for proof-based psychotherapy. New York: Springer, criticize the narcissist (Bushman and Baumeister, 1998) or who socially dismiss the narcissist (Twenge and Campbell, 2003).

Narcissists will likewise discredit the individuals who are reproachful of them (Kernis and Sun, 1994). On group tasks, narcissists rush to reprimand their associates for any disappointment or poor performance, rather than risk taking the blame themselves (Campbell et al., 2000). These relational and psychic examples can be viewed as self-administrative endeavors to support positive perspectives on the self. In that, narcissists are regularly effective, and narcissism in normal populations is associated with higher self-esteem and lower misery and nervousness than other people (Rose and Campbell, in press). There is sparse proof that narcissism is related to success in any direct manner. Almost certainly, narcissism is helpful in specific settings (those supported by certainty and extraversion) and harmful in others (those hampered by overconfidence) (e.g., Wallace and Baumeister, 2002; Campbell, Goodie, and Foster, in press).

The word narcissism gets hurled around a lot in our self-fixated, superstar driven culture, frequently to portray somebody who appears to be unreasonably vain or loaded with themselves. Yet, in mental terms, narcissism doesn't mean self-esteem—in any event, not of an authentic sort. It's increasingly exact to state that individuals with narcissistic character issues (NPD) are fascinated with an admired, gaudy picture of themselves. Furthermore, they're fascinated with this swelled mental self-view absolutely because it permits them to avoid deep feelings of insecurity or weakness. In any case, propping up their dreams of glory takes a great deal of work—and that is the place the broken perspectives and behaviors come in.

Narcissistic personality disorder involves a pattern of egotistical, pompous reasoning and conduct, an absence of sympathy and thought for others, and an over the top requirement for admiration. Others frequently portray individuals with NPD as arrogant, manipulative, narrow-minded, belittling, and requesting. This reasoning and behaving surfaces in each region of the narcissist's life: work and fellowships to family and love connections.

The term narcissism is usually used to describe character qualities among everybody, typically egotistical or looks for consideration. A level of healthy narcissism makes an even, solid character. A narcissistic personality disorder (NPD) is very different and requires explicit criteria that must be met for a conclusion. It only affects a small level of individuals - a more significant number of men than ladies. As portrayed in "Do, You Love a Narcissist?" Someone with NPD is pretentious (sometimes only in fantasy), needs compassion, and requirements profound respect from others, as shown by five of these abridged attributes:

1. An affected feeling of   self-importance and exaggerates accomplishments and talents

2. Dreams of boundless power, achievement, brilliance, beauty, or perfect love
3. Lacks sympathy for the emotions and needs of others
4. Requires over the top profound respect and admiration
5. Believes he or she is exceptional and one of a kind, and must be comprehended by, or should connect with other uncommon or of high-status individuals (or establishments)
6. Unreasonably anticipates uncommon, favorable treatment or consistence with their desires
7. Exploits others to accomplish personal ends
8. Envies others or accepts they're jealous of him or her
9. Has "a mentality" of egotism or acts that way

The disorder differs from mellow to outrageous. In any case, of the considerable number of narcissists, be careful with threatening narcissists, who are the most malignant, antagonistic, and damaging. They take characteristics 6 and 7 to an extraordinary and are evil and noxious.

Individuals with narcissistic personality disorder are remarkably impervious to changing their behavior, in any event, when it's causing them problems. Their propensity is to turn the fault on to other people. They are also amazingly sensitive and react thoughtfully to even the slightest criticisms, disagreements, or perceived slights, which they see as personal attacks. It's regularly simpler for the individuals in the narcissist's life to oblige their requests to maintain a strategic distance to avoid the rage and wraths. However, by seeing progressively about narcissistic personality disorder, you can detect the narcissists throughout your life, shield yourself from their strategic maneuvers, and build up more beneficial limits

The 'narcissistic predicament' is seen while, being condemned, the narcissists show themselves desolately unequipped for holding any emotional balance. But, these upset people likewise offer an abnormally developed ability to blame others. Their dilemma is that the rigidity of their defenses, inability to let their guard down, even among their nearest individuals, ensures that they will never get what they most need, which, unfortunately, they are themselves careless regarding. Individuals have never conceived narcissists; it is ground-breaking natural impacts that make them so. Being disregarded and overlooked, or continually derided or criticized by guardians in youth, they structure ridiculously elevated conduct expectations. Incapable to get together to their folks' wild, stickler desires, they create an imaginary "perfect self" that could get the parental acknowledgment, even admiration, which they long for. The primary components of narcissism are narcissistic supply, narcissistic rage and narcissistic injury, and narcissistic abuse

CAUSES OF NPD

Narcissistic Personality Disorder is in a comparable classification with antisocial or borderline personality disorders, in that the individual who suffers is frequently improperly passionate. The hidden reasons for everyone in this clutter can be intricate and are best comprehended by a professional therapist.

NPD likely has its underlying foundations in a dysfunctional childhood, for example, great spoiling, high standards, and unnecessary recognition. Or then again, the inverse might be the reason for misuse and disregard. NPD sufferers feel they are characteristically awful, disgraceful, and disliked. They were condemned by their folks who neglected to give them friendship. They feel a disgrace about their identity, and because of this absolute disgrace, they are helpless in the world. They attempt to keep that weakness under control by being very controlling and influential. They can't bear to open up because they may be dismissed, and dismissal is disastrous. Their disgrace can't be presented to the world since it is too appalling to contemplate.

The individuals who have NPD frequently seem to function typically at work or in social settings. They can even be profoundly successful as business people or at the nation club. But, their close relationships endure. Here are a few manifestations to look for.

Signs and side effects of narcissistic personality disorder
Those with NPD ordinarily have at any rate a few of these characteristics:

- A feeling of superiority
- Obsession with power, achievement, attractiveness
- A conviction that the person in question is unique and should just connect with other high-status individuals
- A desire for consistent commendation and consideration
- Failure to perceive others' feelings and emotions
- Exploitative of others and utilizations them to accomplish their objectives
- Condescending to those the person he or she feels inferior
- Jealous of others and thinking others are envious of that person

- Arrogant conduct, feeling qualified for need treatment
- Easily hurt and dismissed
- Very delicate self-esteem
- Appearing to be extreme disapproved and dispassionate

Somebody who has these indications will experience issues keeping up good connections.

A bombastic feeling of self-importance Grandiosity is the defining characterizing for narcissism. Something other than egotism or vanity, gaudiness is an unreasonable feeling of superiority. Narcissists accept they are exciting or "exceptional" and must be comprehended by other uncommon individuals. Also, they are unreasonably useful for anything typical or expected. They just need to relate and be related to other high-status individuals, places, and things. Narcissists additionally accept that they're better than every other person and anticipate acknowledgment in that capacity — in any event, when they've done nothing to procure it. They will frequently misrepresent or inside and out lie about their accomplishments and abilities. Furthermore, when they talk about work or connection, all you'll hear is the amount they add to how incredible they are and how fortunate the individuals in their lives are to have them. They are the undisputed star, and every other person is, best case scenario a piece player.

- **Lives in a dreamland that supports their delusions of loftiness**

Since reality doesn't support their grandiose perspective, narcissists live in a dreamland propped up by distortion, self-misdirection, and mystical reasoning. They turn self-praising dreams of boundless achievement, power, brightness, allure, and perfect love that cause them to feel uncommon and in charge. These dreams shield them from feelings of inner emptiness and disgrace, so realities and conclusions that negate them are disregarded or legitimized away. Anything that takes steps to blast the dream bubble is met with extraordinary protectiveness and even rage, so those around the narcissist figure out how to step cautiously around their denial of the real world.

- **Needs steady applause and esteem**

A narcissist's feeling of superiority resembles an inflatable that step by step loses air without a constant flow of commendation and acknowledgment to keep it swelled. Infrequent recognition isn't sufficient. Narcissists need steady nourishment for their sense of self, so they encircle themselves with individuals who are happy to oblige theirs over the top longing for affirmation. These relationships are very one-sided. It's everything about what the admirer can accomplish for the narcissist, never the reverse way around. What's more, if there is ever interference or diminishment in the admirer's consideration and applause, the narcissist regards it as a selling out.

- **Sense of entitlement**

Since they view themselves as exceptional, narcissists expect the right treatment as their due. They genuinely accept that anything they desire, they ought to get. They likewise anticipate that the individuals around them should consequently agree to their every desire and impulse. That is their lone worth. On the off chance that you don't envision and address all their issues, at that point, you're futile. What's more, if you have the nerve to oppose their will or "egotistically" request something consequently, set yourself up for hatred, shock, or the brush off.

- **Exploits others without blame or disgrace**

Narcissists never build up the capacity to relate to others' sentiments — to imagine others' perspectives. They need compassion. From various perspectives, they see the individuals in their lives as items to serve their necessities. As a result, they don't mull over exploiting others to accomplish their closures. Now and then, this relational abuse is malignant, yet frequently it is just unaware. Narcissists essentially don't consider how their conduct influences others. Furthermore, on the off chance that you call attention to it, they despise everything you won't get. The main thing they comprehend is their own needs.

- **Frequently disparages, scares, menaces, or deprecates others**

Narcissists feel compromised when they experience somebody who seems to have something they need — particularly the individuals who are sure and mainstream. They're likewise compromised by individuals who don't kowtow to them or who challenge them in any capacity. Their safeguard system is disdain. The best way to kill the danger and prop up their listing sense of self is to put those individuals down. They may do it in a disparaging or pompous manner to exhibit how little the other individual intends to them. Or then again, they may go on the assault with affronts, verbally abusing, tormenting, and dangers to compel the other individual to go into line.

NARCISSISTIC PERSONALITY DISORDER (NPD) IS A REAL, PATHOLOGICAL MENTAL DISORDER.

The disease is regularly misdiagnosed by the medical community and is quite often disregarded and unrecognized by society. All individuals are narcissistic to a small degree. It is consummately ordinary to love and regard oneself; without such self-respect, humanity would never have developed into a cutting edge society.

The narcissist: extraordinary obsessive self-centeredness, But NPD is a severe distortion of the self-esteem, going amiss generally from ordinary character working. It isn't mistaken for "qualities" or parts of an individual's personality or state of mind. It is an incapacitating, neurotic issue that keeps the narcissist from adding to society and often prompts violent, hostile social conduct towards others.

The narcissist needs sympathy for other people. Given his self-respect, he can't perceive that any move he makes could be inadmissible in the public eye. Disgrace isn't an inclination he ever encounters.

The narcissist has a total failure to recognize that he is blemished; even in circumstances where he is compelled to concede botches, he will, in any case, build expand avocations, regularly inside, which clarify the issues he caused just like the issue of others.

Ineffective companionships and personal connections Because of his absence of compassion for other people, a narcissist seldom has some nearby private fellowships. As far as sentimental connections, he is rarely effective in close, commonly adoring encounters, as he can't acknowledge that someone else's necessities could be as significant as his own.

He is unequipped for comprehension and tuning in to other people. The interests and pastimes of others are non-existent to him. It isn't just that he expects others in his life to share indistinguishable interests from he does; he basically can't fathom that someone else could be keen on an option other than what intrigues him at that point. The narcissist doesn't perceive sentiments in others. The narcissist is so incognizant regarding others' feelings that his passionate insight is regularly that of a little child.

Like a little youngster, he is unequipped for controlling his feelings. He doesn't understand that his sentiments originate from inside and that he can hold his feelings. He proceeds through grown-up existence with the kid like the conviction that outer occasions and individuals are altogether answerable for his states of mind and that he is vulnerable to control himself. This absence of passionate discretion quite often shows itself in wild and brutal emotional episodes. The narcissist can be charming and enjoyment in one moment, but the next moment furious, shouting, and breaking plates.

The narcissist is unequipped for perceiving that his severe emotional episodes are unreasonable, hostile to social and neurotic; whenever squeezed, his ceaseless need to keep up his dream of self-flawlessness will make him legitimize his conduct as the "issue" of outside individuals and occasions. As opposed to society's mixed up comprehension, the narcissist's staggering issue isn't great self-esteem, but instead powerlessness to perceive and cherish others as discrete creatures. To redress, the narcissist makes an over-misrepresented picture of himself, his triumphs, and his significance. Right now is the most outrageous type of hostile to a social, mental issue.

The narcissist needs to control others since he is unequipped for tolerating that his dream of super affectedness isn't valid. At the point when he can't apply his command over others - at the end of the day, when others act as per their own through and through freedom and not as indicated by his impulses and wants - the narcissist can't adapt and regularly will respond by flying into a fury or getting away from the circumstance to protect his distorted feeling of intensity.

Heinz Kohut first broke down the narcissistic anger in the mid-1970s. Narcissism begins in youth; most research shows that obsessive narcissism is certainly not a natural attribute but a disappointment of character advancement.

NPD starts at an early age. One typical reason is parental disregard. In families in lower financial conditions, this shows itself in inside and out disregard of the kid, various hours of the day in which the youngster is unattended and overlooked. In families at exceptionally high financial levels, parental apathy appears as "care-by-babysitter." The kid has next to no contact with his parent(s), frequently not by any means living in a similar house as them, and is raised by an endless stream of live-in caretakers.

Chapter 3: What Is Narcissistic Abuse?

Abuse might be mental, physical, money related, otherworldly, or sexual. Here are a couple of instances of misuse you might not have recognized:

- Verbal misuse: Includes disparaging, harassing, denouncing, accusing, disgracing, requesting, requesting, compromising, condemning, mockery, seething, restricting, undermining, intruding on, blocking, and verbally abusing. Numerous individuals periodically set expectations, use sarcasm, interfere, hinder, reprimand, fault, or square you. Think about the specific situation, hostility, and recurrence of the conduct before marking it as narcissistic abuse.

- Manipulation: Generally, control is a backhanded impact on somebody to carry on to advance the controller's objectives. Regularly, it communicates clandestine hostility. Think about a "two-timer." superficially, the words appear to be innocuous - even complimentary; however, underneath, you feel disparaged or sense an unfriendly goal. You may not remember it all things considered on the off chance that you encountered control growing up.

- Emotional blackmail: Emotional extortion may incorporate dangers, outrage, admonitions, terrorizing, or discipline. It's a type of control that incites questions in you. You feel dread, commitment, as well as blame. You feel the fear, obligation, and guilt sometimes referred to as "FOG."

- Gaslighting: Intentionally making you doubt your impression of the real world or accept that you're mentally incompetent.

- Competition: Competing to be on top, through dishonest methods, for example, cheating in a game.

- Negative contrasting: Unnecessarily making correlations with adversely balance you with the narcissist or others.
- Sabotage: Disruptive obstruction with your undertakings or connections with the end goal of vengeance or individual favorable position.
- Exploitation and objectification: Using or exploiting you for individual finishes without respect for your emotions or requirements.
- Lying: Persistent misleading to dodge obligation or to accomplish the narcissist's ends.
- Withholding: Withholding such things as cash, sex, correspondence, or fondness from you.
- Neglect: Ignoring the requirements of a kid for whom the abuser is dependable. Incorporates kid endangerment, i.e., putting or leaving a kid in a hazardous circumstance.
- Privacy attack: Ignoring your limits by glancing through your things, telephone, mail, denying your physical protection, or stalking or tailing you, disregarding security you've mentioned.
- Character death or defamation: Spreading malignant gossip or lies about you to others.
- Violence: This incorporates obstructing your development, pulling hair, tossing things, or obliterating your property.
- Financial misuse: Financial maltreatment may incorporate controlling you through financial mastery or depleting your accounts through coercion, burglary, control, or betting, or by gathering obligation in your name or selling your property.
- Isolation: Isolating you from companions, family, or access to outside administrations and backing through control, control, offensive attack, character death, or different methods for misuse.

Narcissism and the seriousness of misuse exist on a continuum. It might go from overlooking your feelings to violent aggression. Ordinarily, narcissists don't assume liability for their conduct and move the fault to you or others. As it may, some do and are fit for feeling blame and self-reflection.

DANGEROUS NARCISSISM AND SOCIOPATH

Somebody with increasingly narcissistic characteristics who carries on in a vindictive, threatening way is considered to have "harmful narcissism." Malignant narcissists aren't pestered by guilt. They can be vicious and enjoy inflicting pain and be so competitive, unprincipled that they participate in anti-social behavior. Paranoia puts them in a defensive-attack mode as a method for self-protection.

Unhealthy narcissism can look like sociopathic. Sociopaths have deformed or harmed brains. They show narcissistic characteristics, yet not all narcissists are sociopathic. Their inspirations vary. While narcissists prop up a perfect persona to be respected, sociopaths change their identity to accomplish their self-serving motivation. They have to succeed at all expenses and barely care about overstepping social standards and laws. They don't append to individuals as narcissists do. Narcissists would prefer not to be deserted. They're mutually dependent on others' endorsement; however, sociopaths can walk away from relationships that don't serve them without much of a stretch. Although a few narcissists will appear once in a while plot to get their goals, they're typically more responsive than sociopaths, who coldly calculate their plans.

Chapter 4: What Makes You Vulnerable To A Narcissistic Partner?

There is positively no "type" that a Narcissistic individual will hope to partner up with. They may see you as somebody who will make them look great or feel better. On the off chance that you react to them with a particular goal in mind reliably to take care of their requirement for Narcissistic stockpile, at that point, this conduct will attract them to you. There are qualities in you that you can self-inspect to check whether you have vulnerabilities that draw in Narcissistic people to you.

1. Not realizing what to search for. A Narcissistic individual will generally search for the individuals who see the absolute best in them. For the most part, they will realize how generally will be so "in tuned" with you. It doesn't imply that they are. If you are left reasoning, this is unrealistic. They shower with you with adoration and consideration. They appeared to nearly "read your brain," particularly in the first place. This is so you begin to look all starry eyed at them. At the point when you don't perceive the beginning period's behavior that a Narcissistic individual showcases, you will fall directly into their hands. Better for you to get acquainted with what those signs are and moderate things down from the earliest starting point. Somebody can just cover their conduct for such a long time before their real personality appears.

2. You worry about the concern for bogus obligation in your group of the source. Suppose you have never managed those issues that have obstructed you from your group of beginning. In that case, this is the place you may fall

defenseless against somebody with Narcissistic inclinations. A Narcissistic individual is glad to have you worry about your family's concerns, just as their issues, while not thinking about what you've experienced. You should stand up to and manage issues you've experienced so you are not sucker-punched by being burdened with another person's issues set on you. You can't fix someone else; neither would they be able to improve you. You can decide to manage your problems so they don't keep on being issues that obstruct your future connections. You can likewise place somebody who needs you to convey the duty of their problems and keep away from a toxic relationship much better when you manage your issues first.

3. You are exceptionally empathic. There's nothing amiss with being empathic. It's a magnificent ability you've created. It's when it's uneven; at that point, it is an issue. If you begin seeing, you are frequently expected to listen when an awful show goes on. Yet, when you need somebody to hear you out, the other individual is mysteriously gone. On the off chance that this is a progressing design, be careful. Odds will remain along these lines if you don't utter a word or acknowledge this is alright. You will end up in an uneven relationship. It's additionally a sign you may be associated with somebody with Narcissistic propensities. Try not to overlook those notice signs that something isn't right. Address it at an early stage.

4. You don't communicate, or you decide to quell your very own significant deal needs. It may be the case that you may be revealing to yourself that they need you so that you won't express your very own mess needs. Like number 3, don't disregard this. On the off chance that you attempt to excuse

that it's alright for the time being, it might be that you have to do some self-improvement work. No stable relationship is uneven. Everybody has needs occasionally. You may require somebody to hear you out when you are worried or experiencing an extreme time. On the off chance that you can't converse with that other individual, it's an excellent opportunity to visit; why not.

5. It doesn't feel like an association; they need you to re-parent them. As a whole, we know somebody or see somebody who's "let down their watchman," just to discover them carrying on immaturely. You may hear them state, 'you help me to remember my mom or my dad.' This is certainly not a decent sign. The individual reveals to you that they have unhealed injuring from their mom and father and need to re-make that parent-youngster relationship again to adjust through their uncertain torment. It's not beneficial to be in a parent-youngster relationship where you are the "re-made parent." You'll have a grown-up kid on your hands, not a distributed relationship. This is additionally somebody who's not prepared to be involved with you.

Understand that you will be left with almost no consequence when you decide to proceed with a Narcissistic individual relationship once you perceive all the indications. You will probably be battling disappointment, feel like it's an uneven relationship, and feel unbelievably depleted from it.

In case you're searching for a relationship who will be a genuine accomplice to you, at that point, don't decide to be involved with a Narcissist. These people, shockingly, won't have the option to meet you in a sound association. It's the beginning periods of dating where they turn on the appeal the most. It's acceptable to know the signs sufficiently early and know about what makes you helpless against stop before you get excessively sincerely contributed.

Chapter 5: Narcissistic Relationships

Partners of narcissists feel they conflicted between their affection and pain, staying and leaving; however, they can't do either. They feel neglected, uncared about, and insignificant. When the narcissist is a parent, when their kids arrive at adulthood, the enthusiastic relinquishment, control, and analysis they encounter growing up has adversely influenced their confidence and limit concerning making progress or continuing adoring, personal connections.

Can You Have a Relationship With a Narcissist?

What are we searching for now when we enter a relationship? I am going to deliver this book to ladies because, indeed, most narcissists will, in general, be men. This isn't to state ladies can't carry their issues to a relationship. In any case, ladies are progressively disposed to be Histrionic or have Borderline Personality Disorder, not Narcissistic Personality Disorder or NPD. We should return to thinking about whether you even need to attempt to have a relationship with a narcissist. I surmise you have to comprehend something about narcissism before we examine this inquiry further.

Most importantly, acknowledge narcissistic propensities or narcissistic side effects can happen at a shifting level. As it were, somebody may be diagnosable as having undeniable Narcissistic Personality Disorder. Simultaneously, someone else may show what you'll see alluded to in this book as undesirable, neurotic, or threatening narcissism. Considerably lesser degrees of narcissism can be risky in a relationship.

What number of the criteria for Narcissistic Personality Disorder should a man meet in the Diagnostic and Statistical Manual of Mental Disorders for him to be terrible news for a relationship? I can't respond to that question. Yet, what you have to acknowledge is this: Often, you can be lured or sucked into a relationship with a narcissist, trusting you have recently met your white knight. However, in time, you will understand his reinforcement isn't precisely as gleaming as it initially showed up.

You may be sucked into a relationship with a narcissist since they can be very beguiling. They regularly realize that it will generally be sentimental, and it isn't irregular for the sex to be extraordinary from the outset. At that point, sooner or later, you may come to acknowledge it is increasingly about him. You may feel he needs to give an incredible execution, and you're frequently expected to praise him for a vocation all-around done, as well. What's more, as opposed to feeling nearer to him, instead, you may feel you're turning out to be increasingly more like an item.

No, you don't feel like he genuinely adores you, or he needs just to be with you-however he presumably acted that path to start with. Maybe this shouldn't astonish you, be that as it may. It couldn't be any more obvious, a relationship with a narcissist is actually about him. He regards others as items. He doesn't have must use for others, truth be told, other than for how they may assist him with getting his needs and needs met. What's more, a narcissist relationship may appear to incorporate extraordinary sex from the outset, yet then bit by bit, switch into sexual maltreatment.

The change may be progressive to such an extent that you don't observe reality about what was going on or where you have wound up. Be that as it may, if you stop and consider your sexual relationship with the narcissist, you may well acknowledge you've been doing things that don't speak to you explicitly, however, just to him. They may cause you to feel debased and awful about yourself.

If you are enamored with a narcissist, you may before long feel you're the casualty of his narcissism. However, from the start, you thought you were the most fortunate lady on the planet to have caught the core of this man. In any event, you thought you had seen it, as he maneuvered you into a tornado sentiment and gave you roses and blessings, at that point whisked you off to sentimental excursions. The day will most likely come, notwithstanding, when you moan about the reality, he doesn't bring you blossoms any longer.

In time, you may have numerous grumblings about your relationship with this narcissist, significantly as the haze lifts, and you see things all the more unmistakably. Indeed, you may understand you were conned into deduction; this relationship would have been about stuff. It eventually was most certainly not. You may find it is not a relationship as you characterize the word. Or maybe, it is about you continually stressing over what may please or disappoint him. It is about you doing things that you don't care for, which may even be against your qualities, so far as that is concerned. You are making a decent attempt to satisfy him, and for several reasons, as well. You may accept along these lines, and you can stay away from his narcissistic anger. You likewise trust and ask he will return to acting like the man he was initially.

You shouldn't expect this if you are involved with a narcissist, notwithstanding. Keep in mind, that was a demonstration to suck you in. Presently, however, would he say he is strolling around being his egotistical and pompous self, taking part in psychological mistreatment and boisterous attack that cause your self-esteem to sneak away day by day? Assuming this is the case, you are facing the man he will most likely keep on being. You may have the option to endure a relationship with a narcissist. However, sometime in the future, you have to wake up and ask yourself: Is this how I genuinely need to live? Didn't I say I needed a caring relationship that depended on a healthy organization? Try not to expect that from the man showing undesirable degrees of narcissism. No, recall that he doesn't need to be diagnosed as having undeniable Narcissistic Personality Disorder to make your life hopeless. Also, indeed, isn't life too short to even consider spending it cherishing a narcissist who can't adore you back?

In case you're involved with a narcissist, it's essential to get outside help to see what's happening, revamp your confidence and certainty, and figure out how to impart adequately and set limits. People with Narcissistic Personality Disorder feel that they are a higher priority than others. In addition to the fact that they place themselves on a platform, they think others do likewise. A stable relationship isn't one in which one individual rules over the other; however, these narcissists can't shape sound connections.

A relationship with somebody with Narcissistic Personality Disorder is a single direction road. These relationships are portrayed by verbal and mental maltreatment, putting down, whining, and even physical abuse. Narcissists accept that they can't take the blame no matter what, so any issues with the relationship - and even issues that emerge in everyday living - are the other accomplices' issue. If an error is made, the accomplice is, by one way or another, the one to fault.

The narcissists' requirement for consideration and profound respect leads them to continually search out the individuals who will strengthen their swelled feeling of self-esteem. This means the development of fast connections and long-term accomplice disposal. If the narcissist is hitched, there is a high likelihood that the individual won't be reliable. Usually, if unfaithfulness is found, the accomplice will be to be faulted for not being accurate enough, sufficiently caring, and so forth.

Casualties of a narcissistic abuser regularly show comparable qualities. The most widely recognized is a poor feeling of self-esteem, frequently joined by the powerlessness to settle on choices for themselves. They go through long periods of being informed that they are sufficiently bad, not keen enough, not something enough. After some time, they come to disguise these negative explanations. They question their capacities. This makes them increasingly dependent upon the narcissistic abuser, creating a pattern of codependency.

The individuals who have endured a narcissist account may show any number of passionate and physical side effects that might be hard to credit to the relationship. They are an aftereffect of the pressure they face day by day. These may include disarray, disassociation, poor eating, and dozing propensities, and even indications of Post-Traumatic Stress Disorder (PTSD).

It is incredibly hard for those in a relationship with a narcissist to find support as they have adapted to seeking their abuser for most, if not all, dynamic exercises. Their low feeling of self-esteem makes it simple for them to disregard the possibility that they merit better. Clearly, in their psyches, nobody else would have them. They ought to be content with the relationship they have, despite the way that they are miserable. This is a topic which the abuser will strengthen too.

While troublesome, it is conceivable to get away from the pattern of narcissistic maltreatment. The initial step must be tolerating that nobody merits the steady mortification and requests of the narcissist. As the mental self-view is reestablished to a sound level, it gets simpler to settle on choices without the abuser's information. Usually, this is an incredibly troublesome procedure that may require the assistance of outcasts, including experts. Lamentably, it is normal for narcissistic abusers to confine their accomplices' entrance to other people, particularly the individuals who might communicate conclusions that negate their gaudy feeling of self.

Partners of Narcissists

Partners of narcissists feel double-crossed that the accommodating, mindful, and sentimental individual they began to look all starry eyed at vanished as time went on. They feel concealed and sad and long for the passionate association. They think it's hard to communicate their privileges, needs, and emotions and define limits in differing degrees. The relationship mirrors the enthusiastic surrender and absence of qualification they encountered in adolescence. Since their limits weren't regarded growing up, they're exceptionally touchy to analysis and exposed to narcissistic maltreatment. As their relationship advances, accomplices concede feeling more uncertain of themselves than they once did. Consistently, their confidence and freedom decrease. Some surrender their examinations, profession, leisure activities, family ties, or companions to mollify their partner.

At times, they experience recognitions of the glow and caring from the person they first fell in love-often brilliant, creative, talented, successful, handsome, or beautiful. They don't spare a moment to state that they're focused on remaining in the relationship if just they felt increasingly cherished and acknowledged. For specific individuals, divorce is not an option. They might be co-parenting with an ex, staying with a spouse for parenting or financial reasons, or they need to keep up family ties with a narcissistic or troublesome family member. Some need to leave; however, they do not have the courage.

CHILDREN OF NARCISSISTS

For the most part, narcissistic guardians run the family and can harm their kids' confidence and inspiration. Regularly they endeavor to live vicariously through them. These guardians anticipate greatness and dutifulness and can be severe, jealous, essential, overbearing, or disadvantaged. Although their characters differ, the average factor is that their feelings and needs, especially emotional requirements. As a result, their children learn to adapt, become codependent. They bear the responsibility for meeting the parent's personal needs rather than vice versa.

While their folks feel entitled, they think unentitled and self-sacrifice and deny their own emotions and feelings (except if they, as well, are narcissistic). They don't figure out how to trust and worth themselves and grow up estranged from their actual selves. They might be headed to substantiate themselves to win their folks' approval, yet discover little inspiration to seek after their needs and objectives when not remotely forced (e.g., by a partner, employer, teacher).

Although they might be ignorant of what was absent in their adolescence, a dread of relinquishment and closeness keeps on penetrating their grown-up relationship. They're afraid of making waves or mistakes and being authentic. Many become pleasers used to looking for outer approval, professing to feel what they don't and concealing what they do. By reenacting their family drama, they accept their lone decision is to be distant from everyone else or surrender themselves in a relationship.

Regularly grown-up offspring of narcissistic guardians are discouraged, have unacknowledged annoyance, and feelings of emptiness. They may pull in a junkie, a narcissist, or another inaccessible partner, rehashing the example of enthusiastic deserting from adolescence. , repeating the pattern of emotional abandonment from childhood. Healing requires recovery from codependency and overcoming the toxic shame acquired growing up in a narcissistic home.

Chapter 6: The Narcissist And Her Family

For the most part, we are individuals from a couple of families in our lifetime: the one we are destined to and the one(s) we make. We as real exchange harm, mentalities, fears, expectations, and wants - an entire psychological weight - from the previous to the last mentioned. The narcissist is no particular case.

The narcissist has a dichotomous perspective on humankind: people are either Sources of Narcissistic Supply (and, then, glorified and over-esteemed) or don't satisfy this capacity (and, consequently, are valueless, degraded). The narcissist gets all the adoration that he needs from himself. He needs recognition, proof, deep respect, admiration, and consideration-in of the final analysis, externalized self-limiting ability from the outside.

He does not need, nor does he need to look for affection from relatives or relatives and will not be cherished by children. He gives them a role as the crowd in the performance center of his swelled pretentiousness. He wishes to intrigue them, stun them, compromise them, mix them with wonderment, move them, stand out for them, oppress them, or control them.

He copies and reenacts a whole scope of feelings and utilizes each means to accomplish these impacts. He lies (narcissists are obsessive liars - their exceptionally self is a bogus one). He acts the pitiful, or, its inverse, the flexible and reliable. He paralyzes and sparkles with remarkable scholarly, physical limits and accomplishments, or personal conduct standards increased in value by the family's individuals. When confronted with (more youthful) kin or with his kids, the narcissist is probably going to experience three stages:

From the start, he sees his posterity or kin as a risk to his Narcissistic Supply, for example, considering his life partner or mother. They meddle with his turf and attack the Pathological-Narcissistic-Space. The narcissist makes a valiant effort to disparage them, hurt (even truly), and mortify them. Narcissists ignore the supplies that evoke narcissism, and therefore hate themselves, continue to look at space, magnificent hallucinations, and arrange future troubles, cravings, and harm (Lost Paradise Syndrome). The narcissist responds along these lines to introducing his youngsters or presenting a new focus regarding the family cell (even to another pet!).

Whoever the narcissist sees to be in rivalry for rare Narcissistic Supply is consigned to the adversary's job. The unrestrained expression of hatred and bad atmosphere in this dilemma is incorrect, or unimaginable-narcissists like to stay away. Contrary to beating his offspring or relatives, he disengages from time to time, shrinks inward, becomes cold and uninteresting, or feels dissatisfied with companions. Different narcissists see the open door in the "disaster." They try to control their folks (or their mate) by "assuming control over" the newcomer. Such narcissists corner their kin or their infant kids. Along these lines, in a roundabout way, they profit by the consideration coordinated at the babies. The kin or posterity become vicarious wellsprings of Narcissistic Supply and intermediaries for the narcissist.

A model: by being firmly identified with his posterity, a narcissistic dad makes sure about the mother's appreciative esteem ("What an extraordinary dad/sibling he is"). He likewise accepts some portion of or all the credit for baby's/kin's accomplishments. This is another expansion and penetration process, a system used by narcissists in most of their connections.

As kin or offspring become more established, the narcissist starts to see their capability to be informative, dependable, and good Sources of Narcissistic Supply. His mentality, then, is changed. The previous dangers have now become promising possibilities. He develops those whom he trusts to be the most fulfilling. He urges them to love him, to love him, to be awed by him, to appreciate his deeds and capacities, to figure out how to aimlessly trust and obey him, in short, to give up to his money and to get submerged in his habits degreatness.

At this phase, the danger of kid misuse - up to and including out and out inbreeding - increases. The narcissist is auto-suggestive. He is the favored object of his sexual fascination. His kin and his kids share his hereditary material. Attacking or having sex with them is as close as the narcissist finds a good pace with himself.

Also, the narcissist sees sex as far as an addition. The accomplice is "acclimatized" and turns into an augmentation of the narcissist, a wholly controlled and controlled item. Sex, to the narcissist, is a definitive demonstration of depersonalization and objectification of the other. He strokes off with others' bodies.

Minors present little risk of criticizing the narcissist or confronting him. They are generous, pliant, and bounteous wellsprings of Narcissistic Supply. The narcissist is satisfied with applause, sincere and intellectually substandard, lack of practice, and subordination of the "body" to establish a relationship.

These jobs-jobs assigned to them explicitly, requested, verifiable, and maliciously by narcissists, are best met by those who have not yet fully grown and are at ease. The more seasoned the kin or posterity, the more they become basic, even judgemental, of the narcissist. They are better ready to place into setting and point of view his activities, scrutinize his thought processes, and envision his moves.

As they develop, they regularly decline to keep on playing the thoughtless pawns in his chess game. They hold hard feelings against him for what he had done to them before they were less fit for the opposition. They can check his actual stature, abilities, and accomplishments - which, generally, linger a long way behind the cases that he makes.

This takes the narcissist a full cycle back to the primary stage. Once more, he sees his kin or children/little girls as dangerous. He rapidly gets frustrated and cheap. He lost all his conspiracies. It turns out that he is genuinely far away, missing, and left out. He is unwilling to talk to him. This refers to the pressure of life and the precious and scarce time. He feels troubled, cornered, blockaded, choked, and claustrophobic. He needs to escape, to forsake his duties to individuals who have gotten futile (or in any event, harming) to him. He doesn't comprehend why he needs to help them or endure their organization. He trusts himself to have been intentionally and mercilessly caught.

He either resists inactively (refusing to act or deliberately destroying interpersonal relationships) or rebels effectively (because of being too necessary, strict, horrible, annoying and mentally harsh, etc.). Gradually - to justify his demonstrations to himself - he gets submerged in fear inspired notions with clear distrustful shades.

To his psyche, the individuals from the family plot against him, look to disparage or mortify or subordinate him, don't get him, or hinder his development. The narcissist as a rule, at last, gets what he needs, and the family that he has made deteriorates to his great distress (because of the loss of the Narcissistic Space) - yet in addition to his tremendous help and shock (how might they have given up somebody as exceptional as he?).

This is a cycle: the emergence of new relatives-he destroys the narcissist tries to adapt to, or relatives or offspring-he gets narcissistic supplies from them-he, exaggerates and romanticizes these newly discovered sources-the source changes To be more sophisticated and free, they are hostile to narcissistic behavior-narcissists belittle them-narcissists feel suffocated, and caught-narcissists become suspicious-narcissists rebel and families are broken. This cycle describes not just the family life of the narcissist. It is to be found in different domains of his life (his vocation, for example). Grinding away, the narcissist, at first, feels compromised (nobody knows him, he is no one worth mentioning). Then, he builds up a hover of admirers, comrades, and companions, which he "sustains and develops" to acquire Narcissistic Supply from them. He exaggerates them (to him, they are the most brilliant, the most faithful, with the most incredible opportunities to ascend the professional bureaucracy and different superlatives).

By the way, the narcissist demotes all these recently romanticized people after some enemies of the selfish behavior (essentially commenting, distinguishing, rejecting) challenged him to restrict him.

They thought he was a stupid, weak, eager, talented, and gifted person, which is expected (the most terrible exclamation in narcissist jargon). The immediate purpose is strange. The narcissist feels that he is misallocating his rare and important assets (for example, his time). He feels blockaded and choked. He revolts and emits in a genuine of foolish and pointless practices, which lead to the crumbling of his life.

Destined to assemble and demolish, connect and isolate, acknowledge and deteriorate, the narcissist is unsurprising in his "demise wish." What separates him from other self-destructive sorts is that his desire is conceded to him in little, tormenting portions all through his tragic life.

Chapter 7: 11 Signs you're The Victim of Narcissistic Abuse

Envision this: your whole reality has been twisted and misshaped. You have been savagely abused, controlled, misled, mocked, disparaged, and gas-lit into accepting that you are envisioning things. The individual you thought you knew and the existence you manufactured together has been broken into a million little sections.

Your feeling of self has been dissolved, lessened. You were romanticized, depreciated, at that point, left the pedestal. Perhaps you were even replaced and discarded on various occasions, just to be 'floated' and tricked over into a maltreatment cycle much more unbearable than previously. Possibly you were determinedly stalked, hassled, and bullied to remain with your abuser.

This was no typical separation or relationship: this was a set-up for the undercover and tricky homicide of your mind and feeling of well-being in the world. However, there may not be apparent scars to tell the story; the total of what you have are broken pieces, cracked recollections, and internal battle wounds. This is what narcissistic abuse looks like.

Because of continued abuse, victims may battle with Complex PTSD or PTSD symptoms if they had extra traumas like being mistreated by narcissistic parents/guardians or known as "Narcissistic Abuse Syndrome." The consequence of narcissistic abuse can incorporate anxiety, depression, hypervigilance, a pervasive feeling of toxic emotional flashbacks, shame that relapse the victim back to the abusive occurrences, and overpowering feelings of worthlessness and helplessness.

When we are in an evolving cycle of abuse, it is difficult to accurately determine the situation we are encountering because abusers can stroll through reality to adapt to their needs, participate in serious love collisions after serious incidents, and persuade to be exploited. They are abusers. Suppose you end up experiencing the following 11 symptoms, and you have a toxic, insulting. An abusive relationship with your partner or you have ever had this toxic relationship. In that case, you may just be threatened by a fanatic predator:

1. You experience dissociation as a survival mechanism.

You will feel sincere or even honestly out of touch with your situation, encountering memory, recognition, cognition, and self-perception obstacles. As Dr. Van der Kolk (2015) writes in his book, The Body Keeps the Score, "Separation is the substance of injury. The mind-boggling experience is separated from and divided, with the goal that the feelings, sounds, pictures, musings, and physical sensations take on their very own existence."

Separation can prompt passionate desensitizing even with awful conditions. Brain desensitizing exercises, fixations, addictions, and constraints may turn into a lifestyle since they give you a getaway from your present reality. Your mind discovers approaches to shut out the effect of your agony.

Sincerely, so you don't need to manage the full dread of your conditions.

Likewise, you may create damaged 'internal parts' that become disconnected from the character you occupy with your abuser or friends and family (Johnston, 2017). These inward parts can incorporate the internal identity parts that were never supported, the genuine outrage and nauseating you feel towards your abuser, or parts of yourself you believe you can't communicate around them.

As Rev. Sheri Heller (2015) pointed out, "Integrating and restoring the separated and denied parts of the role usually requires the establishment of strong considerations, taking into account the digestion of enthusiasm, psychological and physical real factors."This inward joining is best finished with the assistance of an injury educated specialist.

2. You walk on eggshells.

A typical manifestation of injury is abstaining from whatever speaks to remembering the damage – regardless of whether it be individuals, spots, or exercises representing that danger. Whether it is your partner, accomplice, relative, colleague, or chief, if you arouse their anger, discipline, or become the object of their jealousy, you will eventually continue to watch what you say or do to this person. Nevertheless, even if the person in question considers you to be qualified to use you as a passionate meditator, you cannot do this even though everything becomes the abuser's target. You become ceaselessly on edge about 'inciting' your abuser in any capacity and may keep away from an encounter or defining limits accordingly.

3. You may also expand the satisfaction of your relatives beyond hurtful sexual relations. When you explore the outside world, especially with individuals who appear to be related to or related to your abuser and abuse, you will lose your freedom or self-assurance Ability. You set aside your fundamental needs and wants, relinquishing your passion and even your physical wellbeing to satisfy the abuser.

You may have once been loaded with life, objective-driven, and dream-arranged. Presently you feel as though you are living just to satisfy the necessities and plans of someone else. Earlier, the narcissist's whole life appeared to spin around you; presently, your real-life rotates around them.

You may have put your objectives, pastimes, fellowships, and individual wellbeing as a second thought just to guarantee that your abuser feels 'fulfilled' in the relationship. Before long, understand that the individual in question will never really be fulfilled, paying little mind to what you do or don't do.

4. You are battling medical problems and physical side effects that speak to your mental disturbance.

   You may have picked up or lost a lot of weight, created genuine medical problems that didn't exist earlier, and experienced physical side effects of untimely maturing. The constant pressure of abuse makes your cortisol levels go too fast; the resistance frame has suffered a significant blow, making you unable to resist physical pain and disease (Germany, 2013).

5. In doing so, you will not be able to rest or experience nauseating nightmares. You will not be able to recall the injury through enthusiastic or visual flashbacks, thereby returning you to where you were injured initially (Walker, 2013). You develop a pervasive sense of mistrust.

   Each individual currently speaks to risk and wind up getting on edge about others' goals, mainly having encountered the evil activities of somebody you once trusted. Your standard alert becomes hypervigilance. Since the narcissistic abuser has endeavored to gaslight you into accepting that your encounters are invalid, you make some hard memories confiding in anybody, including yourself.

6. You experience self-destructive ideation or self-hurting inclinations.

Alongside sorrow and uneasiness may come an expanded feeling of misery. Your conditions feel insufferable, as though you can't get away, regardless of whether you need to. You build up a sense of educated weakness that causes you to feel like you don't wish to endure one more day. You may even take part in self-hurt as an approach to adapt.

As Dr. McKeon (2014), head of the suicide counteraction branch at SAMHSA, notes, casualties of cozy accomplice viciousness are twice as prone to endeavor suicide on various occasions. This is how abusers submit murder wholly and suddenly.

7. You self-disengage.

Numerous abusers disengage their exploited people, yet unfortunate casualties additionally detach themselves since they feel embarrassed about the maltreatment they're encountering. Given the allegations and misjudgments of fanaticism and mental aggression by injured individuals in public, authorized by law, relatives, companions, and personal groups of narcissists may even harm the unfortunate casualties, they may deny their views on abuse. They are afraid that no one will understand or trust them. Therefore, they choose to avoid others instead of seeking help but maintain a distance of judgment and revenge from the abuser. You end up contrasting yourself with others, frequently to the degree of reprimanding yourself for the maltreatment.

A narcissistic abuser is exceptionally gifted at assembling love triangles or carrying someone else into the relationship's dynamic to threaten the person in question additionally. Therefore, casualties of narcissistic maltreatment disguise the dread that they are insufficient and may continually endeavor to 'go after' the abuser's consideration and endorsement.

Exploited people may compare themselves with others in happier, more rewarding relationships or eventually ask their abuser why they seem to respect outsiders more. This can send them down the trapdoor of pondering, "why me?" and stuck in a pit of self-fault. In all actuality, the abuser is the individual who ought to be accused – you are not the slightest bit liable for being manhandled.

8. You self-harm and fall to pieces.

Unfortunately, casualties regularly wind up ruminating over the maltreatment and hearing the abuser's voice in their psyches, enhancing their negative self-talk and propensity towards self-damage. Harmful narcissists 'program' and condition their exploited people to fall to pieces – here and there even to the point of driving them to suicide.

Because of the narcissist's covert and blatant put-downs, boisterous attack, and hypercriticism, unfortunate casualties build up a propensity to rebuff themselves since they convey such harmful disgrace. They may attack their objectives, dreams, and scholarly interests. The abuser has ingrained in them a feeling of uselessness. They start to accept that they are undeserving of beneficial things.

9. You dread doing what you love and making progress.

Since numerous neurotic predators are desirous of their unfortunate casualties, they rebuff them for succeeding. This conditions their exploited people to relate their delights, interests, gifts, and zones of accomplishment with unfeeling and insensitive treatment

Recollect that an extraordinary injury bond is regularly framed among unfortunate casualty and abusers because the victim is 'prepared' to depend on the abuser for their endurance (Carnes, 2015). Exploited people may shield their abusers from legitimate outcomes, depict a cheerful picture of the relationship via web-based networking media, or overcompensate by 'sharing the maltreatment's fault.

11. You protect your abuser and even 'gaslight' yourself.

Rationalizing, minimizing, and denying the abuse are often survival mechanisms for victims in an abusive relationship. To reduce the cognitive dissonance that erupts when someone who claims to love you abuses you, victims of abuse convince themselves that the abuser is not "so bad" or that they must do something to "provoke" the abuse.

By reading up to Narcissistic Personality and Abuse Strategies, you must reduce cognitive dissonance in another direction; thus, you can realize that the narcissist's false self is aware of self-deception than the charming appearance reconciles your current reality. Remember that an intense trauma bond is often formed between victim and abuser because the victim is 'trained' to rely on the abuser for his or her survival (Carnes, 2015). Victims may protect their abusers from legal consequences, portray a happy image of the relationship on social media or overcompensate by 'sharing the blame' of the abuse.

On the off chance that you are now in an oppressive relationship of any sort, realize that you are not the only one regardless of whether you incline. There are a great many survivors everywhere throughout the world who have encountered what you have. This type of mental torment isn't select to any sexual orientation, culture, social class, or religion. The initial step is to be mindful of your circumstance's truth and approve it – regardless of whether your abuser endeavors to gaslight you into accepting in any case.

If you can, a diary about the encounters you have been experiencing to start recognizing the maltreatment's real factors. Offer reality confided in psychological wellness proficient, aggressive behavior at home promoters, relatives, companions, or individual survivors. Start to 'mend' your body through modalities like injury centered yoga and care contemplation, two practices that focus on similar pieces of the mind regularly influenced by injury (van der Kolk, 2015).

Reach out for help if you are experiencing any of these symptoms, especially suicidal ideation. Consult a trauma-informed counselor who understands and can help guide you through the signs of trauma. Make a safety plan if you have concerns about your abuser getting violent.

It is difficult to leave an injurious relationship because of the extreme injury bonds that can create, the impacts of the injury, and the inescapable feeling of vulnerability and misery that can shape because of the maltreatment. However, you need to realize that it is conceivable to leave and start the excursion to No Contact or Low Contact in co-child rearing instances. Recovery from this type of misuse is testing. Yet, it is well worth clearing the way back to opportunity and assembling the pieces around.

Chapter 8: Dealing With A Narcissist

- Don't succumb to the dream: Narcissists can be attractive and beguiling. They are truly adept at making an unbelievable, complimenting mental self-portrait that attracts us. We're pulled in to their apparent certainty and grandiose dreams — and the shakier our confidence, the more enchanting the appeal. It's anything but difficult to become involved with their web, believing that they will satisfy our yearning to feel increasingly significant, progressively alive. In any case, it's only a dream and an expensive one at that.

- Your needs won't be satisfied (or even perceived). Remember that narcissists aren't searching for accomplices; they're searching for submissive admirers. Your sole incentive to the narcissist is as somebody who can reveal to them that they are so incredible to prop up their voracious sense of self. Your wants and emotions don't check.

- Look at how the narcissist treats others. On the off chance that the narcissist lies, controls, damages, and affronts others, the individual will, in the long run, treat you a similar way. Try not to succumb to the dream that you're unique and will be saved.

- Take off the rose-hued glasses. It's essential to recognize the truth about the narcissist in your life, not who you need them to be. Quit rationalizing terrible conduct or limiting the hurt it's causing you. Disavowal won't cause it to leave. Narcissists are incredibly impervious to change, so the genuine inquiry you should pose to yourself is whether you can live like this uncertainly.

- Focus on your fantasies. Rather than losing yourself in the narcissist's fancies, center around the things you need for yourself. What would you like to change in your life? What endowments might you want to create? What dreams do you have to provide up to make an all the more satisfying reality?

- Set sound limits: Healthy connections depend on common regard and mindfulness. Be that as it may, narcissists aren't able to do genuine correspondence in their relationships. It isn't only that they're not willing; they aren't capable. They don't see you. They don't hear from you. They don't remember you as somebody who exists outside of their own needs. Along these lines, narcissists typically damage the limits of others. Additionally, they do as such with a flat the feeling of privilege.

- Narcissists hardly care about their own experiences or acquiring assets, without asking, snooping on your emails and personal letters, listening to discussions, jumping in without saying hello, thinking, and providing you with inadequate assessments and guidance. They may even mention to you what to think and feel. It's critical to see the truth about this infringement, so you can start to make more practical limits where your needs are regarded.

- Make an arrangement. On the off chance that you have a long-standing example of letting others damage your limits, it is difficult to reclaim control. Set yourself up for progress via cautiously thinking about your objectives and the potential obstructions. What are the most significant changes you plan to accomplish? Is there anything you've attempted in the past with the narcissist that worked? Anything that hasn't? What is the perceived leverage among you, and in what capacity will that sway your arrangement? By what method will you implement your new limits? Addressing these inquiries will assist you in assessing your alternatives and build up a practical format.

- Consider a delicate methodology. If saving your relationship with the narcissist is critical to you, you should step delicately. By bringing up their terrible or broken conduct, you are harming their mental self-view of flawlessness. Attempt to convey your message serenely, humbly, and as delicately as would be prudent. Concentrate on how their conduct causes you to feel instead of on their inspirations and expectations if they react with outrage and preventive attempt to avoid panicking. Leave if need be and return to the discussion later.

- Don't set a limit except if you're willing to keep it. You can rely on the narcissist to defy new boundaries and test your cutoff points, so be readied. Catch up with any outcomes determined. You're sending the message that you don't should be paid attention to the off chance you down.

- Be arranged for different changes in the relationship. The narcissist will feel compromised and resentful about your endeavors to assume responsibility for your life. They are accustomed to making significant decisions. To redress, they may step up their requests in different parts of the relationship, separate themselves from rebuffing you, or endeavoring to control or appeal you into surrendering the new limits. It's dependent upon you to stand firm.

- Don't think about things literally: To shield themselves from sentiments of mediocrity and disgrace, narcissists should consistently deny their inadequacies, savageries, and slip-ups. Regularly, they will do as such by anticipating their issues on to other people. It's upsetting to get accused of something that is not your blame or is described with negative qualities you don't have. Be that as it may, as troublesome as it might be, make an effort not to think about it literally. It truly isn't about you.

- Don't get tied up with the narcissist's rendition of what your identity is. Narcissists don't live in actuality, and that incorporates their perspectives on others. Try not to let their disgrace and habitual pettiness undermine your confidence. Decline to acknowledge undeserved obligation, fault, or analysis. That cynicism is all narcissists.

- Don't contend with a narcissist. When assaulted, the regular nature is to protect yourself and refute the narcissist. Be that as it may, regardless of how reasonable you are or how stable your contention, they are probably not going to hear you. Also, contending the point may raise the circumstance in an extremely undesirable manner. Try not to squander your time. Just tell the narcissist you can't help contradicting their appraisal; at that point, proceed onward.

- Know yourself. The best barrier against the put-down and projections of the narcissist is a definite feeling of self. At the point when you know your qualities and shortcomings, it's simpler to dismiss any uncalled for reactions leveled against you.

- Let go of the requirement for endorsement. It's imperative to isolate from the narcissist's feelings and any longing to please or assuage them to the detriment of yourself. It would help if you approved of knowing reality regarding yourself, regardless of whether the narcissist sees the circumstance unexpectedly.

- Look for help and reason somewhere else: If you're going to remain in a relationship with a narcissist, be straightforward with yourself about what you can—and can't—anticipate. A narcissist won't change into somebody who genuinely values you, so you'll have to search elsewhere for passionate help and individual satisfaction.

- Learn what reliable connections closely resemble. You might not have a generally excellent feeling of a stable give-and-take relationship on the off chance you originate from a narcissistic family. The selfish example of brokenness may feel significant to you. Simply advise yourself that as commonplace as it believes, it additionally causes you to feel awful. In an equal relationship, you will feel regarded, tuned in to, and liberated to act naturally.

- Spend time with individuals who give you a legitimate impression of what your identity is. To maintain a point of view and avoid being tied up with the disability of the narcissist, it is essential to invest energy in people who know you and recognize your contemplation and emotions.

- Make new kinships, if essential, outside the narcissist's circle. A few narcissists seclude the individuals in their lives to control them more readily. On the off chance that this is your circumstance, you'll have to put time into remaking past kinships or developing new connections.

- Look for significance and reason in work, chipping in, and interests. Rather than looking to the narcissist to cause you to feel great about yourself, seek practical exercises that utilize your gifts and permit you to contribute.

10 WAYS OF DEALING WITH A NARCISSISTIC PERSONALITY

Here's a look at down to earth approaches to manage somebody who has NPD or narcissistic propensities — in addition to specific tips for perceiving when it's an excellent opportunity to proceed onward.

1. Perceive the truth about them

When they need to, those with narcissistic characters are acceptable at turning on the appeal. You may end up attracted to their unique thoughts and guarantees. This can likewise make them especially famous in work settings. Yet, before you get tempted, observe how they treat individuals when they're not "in front of an audience." Suppose you discover them lying, controlling, or obtrusively disregarding others. In that case, there's no motivation to accept they won't do likewise to you.

Despite what somebody with a narcissistic character may state, your needs and needs are likely immaterial to them. What's more, you might be met with opposition on the off chance that you attempt to raise this issue. The initial phase in managing somebody who has a narcissistic character is essentially tolerating; this is the kind of people they are — there's very little you can do to change that.

2. Break the spell and quit concentrating on them

When there's a narcissistic character in your circle, consideration appears to float their direction. That is my plan — regardless of whether it's antagonistic or constructive consideration, those with narcissistic characters endeavor to keep themselves in the spotlight. You may, before long, wind up getting tied up with this strategy, pushing aside your own needs to keep them fulfilled.

In case you're hanging tight for a break in their consideration looking for the conduct, it might never come. Regardless of the amount you modify your life to suit their necessities, it's never going to be sufficient. If you should manage a narcissistic character, don't permit them to penetrate your feeling of self or characterize your reality. You matter, as well. Normally help yourself to remember your qualities, wants, and objectives.

Assume responsibility and cut out a bit of "personal time." Take care of yourself first and recollect that it's not your business to fix them.

3. Support yourself

There are times while overlooking something or leaving is a fitting reaction — pick your fights, isn't that so?

In any case, a ton relies upon the relationship. For instance, managing a chief, parent, or life partner may call for unexpected methodologies compared to managing a colleague, kin, or kid.

A few people with narcissistic characters appreciate making others squirm. If that is the situation, make an effort not to get noticeably bothered or show inconvenience. That will urge them to proceed.

On the off chance that it's somebody, you'd prefer to keep close in your life, at that point, you deserve to make some noise. Attempt to do this in a quiet, delicate way. You should reveal to them how their words and lead sway your life. Be explicit and steady about what's not adequate and how you hope to be dealt with. However, set yourself up for the way that they may essentially not comprehend — or care.

4. Set clear limits

An individual with a narcissistic character is frequently very self-retained. They may believe they're qualified to go where they need, snoop through your things, or disclose to you how you should feel. Perhaps they offer you intuitive guidance and assume praise for something you've done. Or, on the other hand, constrain you to discuss private things in an open setting.

They may likewise have little feeling of personal space, so they will generally cross any limits. As a general rule, they don't see them. That is the reason you must be inexhaustibly clear about boundaries that are critical to you.

FOR EXAMPLE

Let's assume you have an associate who wants to leave their vast truck such that makes it difficult for you to pull out. Start by immovably requesting that they ensure they leave you enough space. At that point, express the ramifications for not regarding your desires.

For instance, on the off chance that you can't securely retreat, you'll have their vehicle towed. The key is to finish and call the towing organization whenever it occurs.

5. Anticipate that they should push back

If you confront somebody with a narcissistic character, you can anticipate that they should react. When you shout out and set limits, they may return with specific requests of their own. They may likewise attempt to control you into feeling regretful or accepting that you're the one being irrational and controlling. They may make a play for compassion. Beset up to persevere. If you make a stride in reverse, they won't take you truly next time.

6. Recall that you're not to blame

An individual with narcissistic character issue isn't probably going to concede a mix-up or assume liability for harming you. Instead, they will, in general, undertaking their negative practices onto you or another person. You may be enticed to keep the harmony by tolerating fault; however, you don't need to disparage yourself to rescue their self-image. You know the reality. Try not to let anybody remove that from you.

7. Discover an emotionally supportive network:

Suppose you can't stay away from the individual, attempt to develop your reliable connections by meeting with groups of people or individuals to discuss your problems. Investing a lot of energy in a broken relationship with somebody who has a narcissistic character can leave you genuinely depleted. Revive old fellowships and attempt to sustain new ones. Get together with family more frequently. If your group of friends is littler than you'd like, have a go at taking a class to investigate another diversion. Get dynamic in your locale or volunteer for a nearby foundation. Accomplish something that permits you to meet more individuals you feel great with.

WHAT IS A HEALTHY RELATIONSHIP?

Investing a ton of energy with a narcissistic character can make it difficult to recall what a good relationship even feels like.

Here are a couple of signs to search for:

- Both individuals tune in and put forth an attempt to see one another
- Both individuals recognize their missteps and assume liability for them
- Both individuals feel like they can unwind and be their actual selves before the other

Individuals with narcissistic characters are acceptable at making guarantees. They guarantee to do what you need and not to do that thing you hate. They guarantee to by and massive improvement. What's more, they may even be earnest about these guarantees. Be that as it may, no doubt about it: The guarantee is an unfortunate chore for somebody with a narcissistic character. When they get what they need, the inspiration is no more. You can't depend on their activities, coordinating their words. Request what you need and persevere. Demand that you'll satisfy their solicitations after they've met yours. Try not to give in on this point. Consistency will help drive it home.

8. Comprehend that a narcissistic individual may require professional assistance.

9. Individuals with NPD frequently don't see an issue — in any event, not with themselves. But individuals with NPD often have different clutters, for example, substance misuse or other psychological wellness or character issues. Having turmoil might be what prompts somebody to look for help. You can recommend that they connect for professional assistance, yet you can't cause them to do it. It's their obligation, not yours. What's more, recall, while NPD is an emotional wellness condition; it doesn't pardon terrible or oppressive conduct.

10. Perceive when you need assistance

Routinely managing somebody who has a narcissistic character can negatively affect your own psychological and physical wellbeing.

When to proceed onward

A few people with a narcissistic character can likewise be obnoxiously or sincerely injurious. Here are a few indications of an oppressive relationship:

- Name-calling, affronts
- Patronizing, open embarrassment
- Yelling, compromising
- Jealousy, allegations

Other admonition signs to look for in the other individual include:

- Blaming you for everything that turns out badly
- Monitoring your developments or endeavoring to separate you
- Telling you how you truly feel or should feel
- Routinely anticipating their inadequacies onto you
- Denying things that are evident to you or endeavoring to gaslight you
- Trivializing your assessments and requirements

However, when is it an opportunity to quit? Each relationship has its high points and low points, isn't that so? While this is valid, it's commonly best to leave the relationship if:

- You're by and large obnoxiously or genuinely mishandled
- You feel controlled and controlled
- You've been indeed abused or feel compromised
- You feel disconnected
- the individual with NPD or a narcissistic character gives indications of psychological sickness or substance misuse, however, won't find support
- Your mental or physical wellbeing has been influenced

Chapter 9: Narcissist Abuse Syndrome

An individual deceived by narcissistic abuse frequently comes to counseling and oblivious and disconnected from her emotional pain and mental anguish. Instead, she usually focuses on disappointment, insufficiency, and frantic search for the best solution to a particular problem, the narcissist believes that narcissism is the cause of his pain. He may even make her unable to meet the desire for treatment, a large part of which is because she does not have enough mindfulness, over-care for children or family, as well as unsatisfactory sex life, then she dreams of sex.

- The ideological design of casualties caused by narcissistic abuse is often full of self-negligence and self-judgment. For example, at the beginning of the treatment and even in the later stages, she often provided some expressions over and over again, accompanied by: "We truly have no issues, simply minor things."
- "We're cheerful and get along more often than not!"
- "It truly is all me."
- "Can you fix me, please?"
- "Can you make me quit upsetting him to such an extent?"
- "I don't' have any desire to lose him. Would you be able to fix me?"
- "After what I did, how might I request that he love me?"
- "Is there trust in me?"

In expansion to redundant articulations, her reasoning and words depict the issues she faces with an imbalanced awareness of others' expectations. For instance, she:

- It is "fizzling" to cause him to feel cherished and make sure about it.
- "Can't make sense of" how to fix herself to quit upsetting him.
- Can't censure him for grilling her, being reformatory, sulking, disregarding her, hollering, verbally abusing, and so on.
- Did things that "so squashed him" he'll never get over, although "it's minor things."
- She doesn't comprehend why she opposes at least one of his requests, i.e., to concur she's "insane" and "needs prescriptions."
- Is the reason for his issues with other ladies.

The casualty of narcissistic abuse feels and contemplates herself, life, and the narcissist, in many territories, mirrors a few or more noteworthy degrees what the narcissist needs her to think, accept, feel, this is what "emotional manipulation" is and looks like. The term should be held for narcissistic abuse, particularly from language utilization, such as coercing, dangers, verbally abusing, and disgracing. So forth, while sincerely oppressive, most people use (to incorporate casualties of narcissists)to some degree. Most have encountered firsthand in youth (these practices are tragically still generally viewed as typical in youngster raising). Though enthusiastic control has violent means to take another's psyche and will hostage, genuinely oppressive language (also unsafe!) is established in programmed reactivity that is fundamentally guarded and defensive.

Likewise, this qualification is imperative to incapacitate the strategies of narcissists who plans, covertly and overtly, to stow away and fault move the names of "narcissist" and "genuinely manipulative" onto their unfortunate victims.

Narcissist abuse syndrome shows a considerable lot of the side effects of posttraumatic stress issue (PTSD), to include:

- Intrusive contemplations or recollections

- Physical-enthusiastic responses to tokens of injury
- Nightmares and flashbacks (feeling as though the occasion is going on once more)
- Avoidance contemplations, individuals or circumstances related to the injury
- Melancholic musings about self and world
- Distorted feeling of accuse identified with injury
- Sense of separation or detachment from others
- Difficulty concentrating and, or dozing
- Hyper-watchfulness, touchiness, effectively frightened

THE NATURE AND EFFECTS OF NARCISSISTIC ABUSE

If you have experienced narcissistic abuse, then understanding the concept of narcissistic abuse, its effects, and the narcissistic abuse syndrome are essential to repair and rebuild the ability to participate in self-care. The principle distinction between an NPD and APD is a line the NPD doesn't cross. Neither express regret for abuse or harm to others. However, contrary to narcissists, social perversions far exceed those from the legal exploitation of others to illegal exploitation, physical abuse, economic exploitation, etc. In their mind, those in status positions should demonstrate they're calloused, show no sympathy. In a couple of relationships, incurring pain is respected a custom right by both NPDs and APDs, likened to preliminary rehearses in elite gatherings for men, i.e., cliques, mystery social orders, sports groups.

Both enjoy harming and abusing others for their benefit — with no regret. No regret goes with the job. Remorse and compassion are for powerless, second rate, low-status people.

A narcissist stays powerless and delicate and snared on demonstrating human love. Common caring is fake, to the extent that he will not recognize that he's human. Each person is wholly outfitted with assets and insight — and that it's challenging to control another individual, even youngsters, without significant expense to self.

The human brain has mirror neurons. To the extent, one feels disdain, contempt, scorn for another, one's body creates the neurochemical perspectives and body inside themselves. It's incomprehensible for a person to try to hurt another without harming themselves deliberately.

In a dumbfounding manner, the mutually dependent remains likewise snared on empowering the narcissist, as narcissist supply. There is a critical contrast in any case! In contrast to the narcissist, she has not lost her association with being human! She is lost in a fantasy deception, which prevents her from getting rid of the belief that soon, to some extent, her worship and penance will turn an undeniable abuser into one who can see And think about the sovereign. Her emotions along these lines, moderately, there's no correlation! She's the sound one, basically because: she longs to realize how to adore — that is human, and it doesn't beat that! The genuine issue, and in that lies the arrangement is to break liberated from "lethal gentility" standards that don't give her authorization to love and regard herself as a vital establishment love another.

Love is an activity, moderate activity. Certified love cultivates both self and the other entire creatures' development and prosperity, equipped to give and get love. Nothing is a higher priority than leaving the mist and dreams of dangerous codependency to feel invigorated once more.

Chapter 10: Long Term Damages To The Victims

Neuroscience:
The shocking effect narcissistic abuse has on the brain. The impacts of mental and narcissistic abuse accompany many obliterating results. Yet, there are two that practically nobody thinks about–except if they're a specialist or neuroscientist.

In the long run, these two results may be the most devastating consequences of emotional trauma and are another motivation for you to try to leave under reasonable circumstances when your child has a narcissistic partner. At this point, most of us realize that rehashed enthusiastic injury prompts both PTSD and C-PTSD, which ought to be reason enough to leave an abusive partner. But, what a large number of individuals don't understand is that after some time, these rehashed emotional wounds contract the hippocampus, which is answerable for memory and learning, while at the same time extending the amygdala, which houses crude feelings, for example, dread, distress, blame, jealousy, and disgrace.

Hippocampus essentials

The hippocampus, which is Greek for "seahorse," is a combined structure tucked inside every transient flap and formed, truth be told, similar to a couple of seahorses. It assists with putting away and discharge memory. The hippocampus is particularly crucial for instantaneous memory, making it the main focus of several pieces of information for a few seconds, and then moving it to permanent memory or immediately ignored. Learning relies upon short memory.

Further, among the numerous investigations that have been led, one specifically shows extremely upsetting outcomes. In a study directed by a group of the University of New Orleans and Stanford University analysts, patients with the most noteworthy pattern cortisol (a pressure hormone) and a more prominent number of PTSD side effects had the best abatements in hippocampal volume after some time.

The more you remain with a sincerely oppressive accomplice, the more crumbling you can expect of your hippocampus. It can be seen very well how this neurological method can improve the sense of casualties caused by narcissism and psychotic abuse, emotional disharmony, and abuse of amnesia.

Amygdala fundamentals

Narcissists keep their unfortunate casualties in a steady condition of nervousness and dread, making their exploited people respond from their amygdala (or "reptilian" cerebrum). The amygdala controls life capacities, for example, breathing and pulse and the essential feelings of affection, hate, dread, and desire (which are all thought to be "basic feelings").

It's additionally answerable for the battle or flight response. Casualties of narcissistic maltreatment live right now every day. After some time, the amygdalae recollect the things we felt, saw, and heard each time we had an agonizing encounter. In this unpleasant situation, subconscious traces will trigger organ attacks or escape schedules, thereby keeping people away from practice or introverted conflict (another practical reason is to avoid harassment through the predecessor of web-based online media you). Significantly after the toxic relationship has finished, exploited people endure PTSD, C-PTSD, alarm assaults, fears, and the sky is the limit from there... because of the activating of their raw feelings of trepidation by their overactive amygdalae. Out of these feelings of nervousness, focuses of narcissistic maltreatment frequently take part in crude safeguard components including (yet not restricted to):

- Denial – Victims use denial to escape from painful feelings or areas of their life they don't want to admit.

- Compartmentalization – Victims pigeonhole the abusive aspects of the relationship to focus on the positive aspects.

- Projection – Victims project their traits of compassion, empathy, caring, and understanding onto their abuser, when, in fact, narcissists and other emotional abusers possess none of those traits.

Narcissistic Abuse Changes Your Brain
According to Goleman (2006), everything we learn, everything we read, everything we do, everything we understand, and everything we experience counts on the hippocampus to function correctly. "The continual retention of memories demands a large amount of neuronal activity.

The cerebrum's creation of new neurons and setting down associations with others happens in the hippocampus" (Goleman, 2006, p. 273). Goleman likewise expressed, "The hippocampus is particularly defenseless against continuous enthusiastic pain, given the harming impacts of cortisol."

When the body perseveres through progressing pressure, cortisol influences the rate at which neurons are either included or subtracted from the hippocampus. This can have grave outcomes in learning. When the neurons are assaulted by cortisol, the hippocampus loses neurons and is diminished in size. A span of pressure is nearly as dangerous as excessive pressure. Goleman clarified, "Cortisol animates the amygdala while it impedes the hippocampus, compelling our consideration onto the feelings we feel while confining our capacity to take in new data."

Goleman includes, The neural expressway for dysphonia runs from the amygdala to the right side of the prefrontal cortex. As this hardware enacts, our contemplations focus on what has set off the misery. What's more, as we become a distracted state, our psychological dexterity sputters with stress or disdain. Similarly, when we are pitiful, movement levels in the prefrontal cortex drop, and we produce less contemplation. Boundaries of uneasiness and outrage from one viewpoint and trouble on the other push mind movement past its zones of adequacy. But, there is hope. You can do reparative activities to restore and rebuild your hippocampus and stop your psyche's hijacking by your amygdala.

What to do

Fortunately, as cerebrum examines have now appeared (because of the enchantment of neuroplasticity), it is feasible for the hippocampus to regrow. A powerful strategy incorporates the utilization of EMDR treatment (Eye Movement Desensitization and Reprocessing). One ongoing examination demonstrated that 8 to 12 meetings of EMDR for patients with PTSD indicated a normal of a 6% expansion in the volume of their hippocampi.

EMDR is likewise helpful for checking the amygdala's hyper excitement, permitting the cerebrum to all the more suitably direct what requirements to happen instead of staying stuck and pointlessly triggers complicated feelings.

Chapter 11: Step By Step Instructions To Leave A Narcissist

Cutting off an oppressive association is rarely straightforward. Done with a narcissist is particularly troublesome because they are so charming and charming-in any case, whether it's at the beginning of the relationship or by chance when you take steps to leave. It's anything but difficult to get perplexed by the narcissist's manipulative conduct, made up for a lost time in the need to look for their endorsement, or even to feel "gaslit" and uncertainty your judgment. In case you're mutually dependent, your craving to be faithful may best even your need to protect your security and feeling of self. Yet, it's essential to recollect that nobody has the right to be harassed, undermined, or obnoxiously and genuinely manhandled in a relationship. There are approaches to get away from the narcissist—and the blame and self-fault—and start the way toward mending.

- Educate yourself about narcissistic disorder. The more you comprehend, the better you'll have the option to perceive the methods a narcissist may use to keep you in the relationship. At the point when you take steps to leave, a narcissist will regularly revive the blandishment and worship ("love besieging") that made you keen on them in any case. Or then again, they'll make fantastic guarantees about changing their conduct that they do not expect to keep.
- Write down the reasons why you're leaving. Determining why you must disconnect can help you avoid getting into trouble. For example, put the lost information in a convenient place

on your phone and make unique guarantees when you raise self-problems or appeals from a narcissist.

- Seek support. The narcissist may have harmed your associations with loved ones or restricted your public activity during your time together. Be that as it may, whatever your conditions, you're not the only one. Whether you can't contact old companions, you can discover help from help gatherings or abusive behavior at home helplines and sanctuaries.

- Don't make void dangers. It's a superior strategy to acknowledge that the narcissist won't change and when you're prepared, essentially leave. Making dangers or declarations will caution the narcissist and empower them to make it increasingly hard for you to escape.

- Leaving a narcissist can have a significant impact on their seniority and self-esteem. In any case, their immense self-awareness should be taken care of, so they will often try to exert authority on you. Suppose appeals and "love bombardment" are unlikely to work. In that case, they may become dangerous, making you nauseous with familiar companions and colleagues or stalking you through web-based online media or face-to-face. Cut off all contact with the narcissist. The more you get in touch with you, the more expectation you'll give them that they can reel you back in. It's more secure to hinder their calls, messages, and messages and detach from them via web-based networking media. If you have youngsters together, have others with you for any planned guardianship handovers.

- Allow yourself to lament. Breakups can be amazingly intricate, whatever the conditions. In any event, cutting off a lethal association can leave you feeling dismal, angry, baffled, and lamenting the loss of shared dreams and duties. Recuperating can require some serious energy, so back off yourself and go to loved ones for help.

- Don't expect the narcissist to share your troubles. When information penetrates, and you will no longer take care of their self-awareness, the narcissist may continue to abuse others soon. They will not feel miserable or blamed but always demand recognition and deep respect. This is not a reflection of you but a description of the consistent imbalance in their connection.

Chapter 12: Simple Rules When Divorcing A Narcissist

Whether you have been trapped for five days or fifty years, it is difficult to imagine that the person you are separated from today is a similar person who once vowed to engage in endless worship. As the adage goes, the very characteristics that made you hopelessly enamored with an individual are identical qualities that made you drop out of affection toward the relationship's finish. When you are entangled with a narcissist, the separation of legality, budget, and passion becomes increasingly chaotic. Break from people with narcissistic personality problems or even narcissistic orgasms may have been a long time ago. If you allow yourself to fall into their whirlpool, it is a lengthy and laborious problem (no joking plan). Here are eight reasonable and reasonable advancements that you can base on your position, not separate from your own. Decide whether your Ex is a Narcissist.

Your ex may be arrogant, wanton, intestinal, or self-harming, but this does not make the person in question a narcissist. Narcissists are known for lack of compassion and intolerance-not a little bit anyway. People who need to know will not be frustrated by cats they encounter, families that are losing their pets, or unlucky children regardless. They will blame the family for letting the kitten meander, don't blame the cat for escaping the road. Otherwise, they will blame the family, accusing them of expecting to wash the murder on the wheel from the wheel. Presently envision asking the individual who is at the focal point of their universe for a separation. It is safe to say that they will have any knowledge to think about what welcomed this on, or what practices of theirs drove you to this choice? Likely not. Is it true that they will work with you to co-parent the youngsters and cause them to feel sheltered and make sure about the progressions and vulnerability in their lives? Most likely not. Regardless of whether they undermined you, they will reprimand you for making them cheat. Irrespective of whether they genuinely or genuinely attacked you, you're the person who caused them to do it. They will depict themselves as the person in question; they will attempt to make you pay.

When you decide and acknowledge how you are managing a narcissist, your watchman must be up. It would help if you recognized that they would be remarkably hard to work in a separation regardless of whether it is a youngster in question or the steak blades. You can execute them despite everything they will follow you.

1. Spare Rational Thoughts for The Right Audience.

Carrying sound contemplations into any discussion with a narcissist resembles bringing a squirt firearm to a blade battle. Sane considerations are to the narcissist what vegetables are to a little child, feed them as much as you need, they will simply let it out. As much as the baby needs dessert and will pitch a fit to get it, the narcissist wouldn't like to hear you; they simply need to win. They need vindication to show the world they were correct! Their fits of rage come as diversions, intended to keep you cockeyed, occupied, and in guarded mode. You can state, "I need essential care of the children since you misuse liquor." The narcissist will answer, "I can't confide in you with the children since you laid down with our child's soccer mentor." While you're using vitality clarifying that you never met the soccer mentor and his allegation says nothing regarding your capacity to parent, it's past the point of no return. You've just taken the trap. You are examining their favored theme (your failure to parent) versus yours (their capacity to parent). Instead of contending with your ex, serenely and judiciously converse with your attorney and let them talk for your sake.

2. Contract a Divorce Attorney That Specializes in Narcissists.

On the off chance that you claim a Tesla electric vehicle, you're not going to take it to a technician with practical experience in ignition motors. A similar rationale applies to lawful portrayal; not all separation lawyers are made equivalent. Some are acceptable moderators. Others are loudmouthed, forceful sharks. In any case, the court's narcissist strategies require some knowledgeable people to craft a technique to make your separation, especially the nursing process, through legal procedures.

3. Know the Road Ahead.

If you have youngsters, you should persuade an assortment of individuals, each with their motivation and predispositions, that you are the parent best prepared to think about your kids. Your crowds incorporate advocates, specialists, and judges. At each progression, the narcissist will attempt to demonstrate you're lopsided, bumbling, and a risk to your youngsters. Recall the old film "Gaslight?" Suppose you respond genuinely to any allegation during these procedures. In that case, regardless of how silly, you're playing into the picture of you they've produced. Expect the sudden and the most exceedingly terrible conduct from your ex, and you can't be knocked cockeyed or astonished.

4. Record. Spare. Document. Offer.

For the ex, it is usually simple to change the instant message, email, or voice message sent to your lawyer and then send it to his lawyer as evidence against you. The best way to deal with their case is to give the first message sent, which includes a screenshot from the phone, the "sent message" in the email outbox, and a chronicle of all the voices let them know. The ideal way to monitor this issue is to limit contact with your ex and avoid all prospects of the person suspected of inciting you. For example, at a PTA meeting, witnesses can review your actions and non-statements.

On the off chance that you see evidence of their terrible judgment, violent conduct, or maltreatment via web-based networking media, catch it before you petition for legal separation. In any case, your ex can erase the culpable posts, or their records, surprisingly fast.

6. Have a Plan, Stick to It.

You will probably sensibly partition your benefits and duties, so you and your youngsters can push ahead with your lives. For your young people, this arrangement may be with your ex, regardless of whether your ex is the pinnacle of a narcissist. For you, it includes the meagerness allowed in contact with your ex. In that case, the narcissist sees things unexpectedly. For them, its successor is lost to them, but not to you. Any remittances you receive are considered personal sabotage, so they will save you any expenses that will take you off the target. Regardless of whether they paid a legal fee of $50k to protect you from obtaining a vehicle of $25k, no matter what measures you take, you can get the car. They will feel protected in their activities because they can accuse The judge who requested the trial and did not possess any property — official conclusion. Truth be told, the appointed authority's choice may fuel their saint complex for quite a long time to come, which is a triumph for the narcissist. As a feature of your arrangement, recognize what you're willing to surrender; however, request that everything gets isolated similarly when you initially talk about a settlement so the narcissist feels the individual in question denied you something you truly needed when it was a concession any judicious individual would have made on Day #1.

7. Circle the Wagons.
In the Wild West, a train could best guard all individuals against an assault by revolving around the wagons and battling from all sides. While separating from a narcissist, you can hope to be hit from all points and caught off-guard when you wouldn't dare to hope anymore. By encircle yourself with close relatives, companions, and advisors, you won't have to fight your ex alone.

8. Excuse Yourself.

Returning to where we started, it is difficult to envision why you wedded a narcissist at any point. Excuse yourself. Narcissists, naturally, need to succeed at all expenses. During your romance, you were the prize. Therefore, problematic individuals may pile up on appeals, emotions, gender, and confirmations to secure yourself and prevent others from staying with you. Their sure, beguiling, can-do, "in every case close the deal" demeanor may be a piece of what pulled in you to the person in question in any case. After making a deal, completing arrangements, and earning your admiration, narcissists change-and often turn their considerations into different awards and goals (from work progress and betting to sports cars and sweethearts). This cold and determined move will, in the long run, lead you to request a separation. It doesn't matter you didn't see it this time-but. Now you realize that if you are looking for another, more valuable accomplice, you need to pay special attention to narcissistic behavior. Do Some Pre-Divorce Reconnaissance (on the off chance that you have this favorable position of prescience)

Time to channel your inward covert operative ninja and get together, however much intel as could reasonably be expected.

Make duplicates (or take photos). That way, you'll have verification when resources 'disappear' on lasting get-aways to outlandish seaward areas after you record.

Here is a concise rundown of what to report:

- Bank Accounts (joint and sole)
- Documents relating to Real Property
- Mortgages and Lines of Credit
- Recent Pay Stubs
- Tax Returns – recent years least
- Insurance desk work
- Vehicle enlistments/title
- Valuable Antiques/Art/Jewelry

- Investment Accounts
- Retirement Accounts
- Birth declarations, marriage endorsement, Passport

Open an "Armageddon Fund" BEFORE Divorcing a Narcissist: Stash That Cash!
Do what you should to bury some distraught cash. Start a very long time previously if you can.
Open your mystery account with an arbitrary bank, one neither of you has utilized previously. You can set the record to have little correspondence or set it up with a mystery email address. Try not to try and get an ATM card or checks, excessively hazardous.
Put in somewhat to a great extent, gradually, however reliably, every piece includes.

Sell adornments and extravagance endowments on the off chance that you should. I exceedingly prescribe this for the individuals who remain at homes and are reliant on their life partner for all payments.
You're going to require this store when your controlling narcissistic life partner goes primate and attempts to 'smoke you out' through removing the cash.
What's more, don't stress, you can't be blamed for taking. Simply advise your legal counselor the amount you have saved, and it very well may be treated as network property while partitioning resources. Consider it is acquiring.
Additionally, you'll need retainers for legal advisors and other separation experts like a Divorce Financial Analyst-which I likewise enthusiastically suggest!

Have a go at Working with a Divorce Coach
Not going to gloss over it-Divorcing a Narcissist is terrible. Once in a while, we need a little hand-holding; however, you need a real existence preserver.

The ideal deliverer could be a Divorce Coach. It's challenging to settle on life-changing choices under pressure. A Divorce Coach can help you remain intelligent and settle on critical decisions, uninfluential by your emotional coercion.

You could utilize their recommendation as a shield.
It resembles the following: 'Sorry Ex NPD (their name here), my specialist says I have to set up solid fringes so you can't shout and revile me out any longer physician's instructions" click (reviling proceeds on his/her finish of telephone line). Try not to shoot the dispatcher!
I could have utilized one to walk me through fits of anxiety, or whatever those terrible, narcissist-initiated scenes were. You need to endure this crucial step; at that point, you're free (ish).

Take Extra Special Care of Yourself
Facing your narcissistic prospective ex-companion is an everyday fight, and it causes significant damage.
To remain quiet and stable, for yourself and your friends and family, be the other sort to yourself. I did everything from yoga, Reiki, and day by day contemplation. If you've never intervened, NOW is an ideal opportunity to begin.
The words and activities can leave enduring harm on the individuals in their way toward self-magnification and privilege. Try not to let them bring you down.
Be strong and comprehend that their words are simply clamored. They are pitiful and upset creatures who have a considerable amount of work to do on themselves, considerably more than you-their focused on the casualty. I don't envy them.

Understand that You Are Not the Problem and Never Were

While you may feel exploited, it's imperative to realize you were rarely meriting the unsafe and injurious treatment narcissists give out.

Usually, think about how Mr. Perfect loves you deeply with friendship, blessings, and self-esteem during his "pursuit" stage, turning into this callused, scheming, tricky beast you married you? Thinking back, clearly, there were warnings from the beginning, yet they weren't too evident at that point. The evilest of reprobates once in a while publicize their malice. The 'great' ones will go undetected until now, and again it passed the point of no return. You're in too far, for example, hitched to one.

How would you shield yourself from a narcissist on the off chance that they're bosses of the mask and slip into your life unnoticed? First off, whenever around, date somebody for more – in any event, 2.5 years. Furthermore, notice any admonition signs, don't thoroughly brush them away or figure you can transform them.

At that point, take a hard, long search inside yourself. Frequently, a narcissist's survivor is inclined with a mentality that appears to welcome these dangerous connections. A narcissist's casualty could have one, or all, of these three highlights: hyper-dynamic connection. The great need for it will be ideal if you and is a brutal self-pundit. The recuperating procedure is the answer for these blemishes. Narcissists resemble sharks who smell blood in the water; They look for casualties without much investment. Accomplish oneself work to guarantee you'll never fall prey to a narcissist until the end of time.

Perhaps they helped you out over the long haul. Beneficial encounters, even awful ones, drive us to learn essential exercises and develop. Work, however, the experience, and you will turn out a superior, more profound, savvier individual for it. It might be said, and you can thank your bad dream past for an outstanding future-a, narcissist-free future.

Chapter 13: The 7 Things You Must Do While Healing After Narcissistic Abuse

There are approaches to quickly track your recuperating journey and maintain a strategic distance from the impasses and detours that throw you off the path, deferring your inevitable arrival to emotional freedom from your torment/pain.

1. Unfollow. Unfriend. Block. Delete.

Internet-based life often referred to as social media, is the enemy of the rehabilitation process. And not only your predecessor. You must exit boarding, but anyone (enabler, flying monkey, guardian) can ruin your day by helping you remember the pain. You might think what your ex was doing (or doing), which is fascinating, masochistic, and it will make your vehicle scream directly from the cliff to the bottom of the ravine. The reason is that the narcissist will perform one of two actions on social media: They will release a new fabulous life to show happiness without you (no, they want to let the shame in their hearts disappear), or they will bomb you to rejoin in a way that pleads with you, and promises that they will change (only Reference: Narcissists will not modify, they will only worsen). There is a simple method to avoid this nightmare: unfriend, unfollow, block, delete.

2. Enable yourself through your instruction.

Such vast numbers of casualties of narcissistic abuse don't understand they are unfortunate casualties until some other time or considerably after the relationship closes because of an absence of information on what establishes misuse and precisely a narcissist is. I had never known about narcissistic character issues or narcissistic maltreatment. I accepted that a narcissist was simply somebody who glanced in the mirror a ton and took too many selfies. This notwithstanding how I didn't have wounds or broken issues that remain to be worked out for my agony disregarded me feeling secluded and unfit as I was to make sense of what was happening.

When I started to coach myself on what troubles I was experiencing and realized everything about narcissists and their long-term abuse, I could give a name to my grief and understand that I am not all the lunatic thinking about it. Instructing yourself on your experience is significant because you can't name the issue, then you can't fix the problem. It's additionally one more advance to reclaiming the force from the person who hurt you, which implies one more advance toward forward and keeping that vehicle of yours out and about with your foot on the gas.

3. Get rid of the individuals who are not 100% on your side.

This an extreme one, if merely because it's consistently the individuals we wouldn't dare to hope anymore wind up abandoning us in our hour of need. Yet, listen to this: keeping individuals who are in any capacity whatsoever keeping you away from your progress ahead is a sure-fire approach to hinder you from three stages for each two that you take.

At the moment of recovery, you are delicate and full of passion. For those individuals who have no ultimate benefit at all, you will be sensitive, defenseless, and straightforward.

Not sure how to separate who precisely these individuals are? (Cautioning: it could be your dearest companion — or who you thought was a companion — or a relative) Ask yourself this inquiry: When you're with them, do you leave their quality resting comfortable thinking about yourself? Or, on the other hand, more regrettable? Do you have a sense of security with them?

Or on the other hand, do you have a feeling that you need to safeguard yourself? That is all you have to know. Somebody who is totally on your side will have your eventual benefits on a fundamental level, not their own. In this manner, you will feel great when you're around them. Those are the individuals worth keeping. Those are the ones who you need in the rearward sitting arrangement of that vehicle you're driving and who will support you the whole way.

4. Try not to shut out the past.

This endeavor will be four punctured tires on your street to recovery. Although more than likely it will be the hardest thing you'll ever do in your life, you must invest energy considering the past and analyze how you found a good pace is currently. This doesn't mean assuming any fault for what occurred you by a narcissistic abuser because nobody has the right to be manhandled. Nobody "asks" for it. It means, in any case, that you have to make sense of how you wound up with somebody who didn't regard you as you have the right to be treated throughout everyday life and why you set up with it.

I saw this as the hardest piece of mending since I needed to glance back at my youth and my harsh dad. They standardized maltreatment in our family along these lines setting me up when I went out at 18 years old for a future with injurious men. I discovered this was the reason I had no self-esteem. Subsequently, I have no restrictions. Therefore, I don't know that I should get something better than someone who treats me like my father — as an object of his control, just like a person who hasn't changed anything. Following these principles, I should be grateful that any man needs her.

As it happened, I never went back in time to understand all this, so I took a bet and later established an intimate relationship. I generally hear the past in the voice of Alex, the abandoned admirer of Michael Douglas in the film Fatal Attraction: "I'm not going to be overlooked, Dan." When she is disregarded, she goes all blade using insane and attempts to slaughter him, and no one needs that.

5. Do not date or start a new relationship.

The most noticeably awful error one could make while attempting to mend after narcissistic maltreatment is to discover another person to lick their injuries. The explanation is that while you're trying to make sense of what occurred to you and unravel yourself from the snare of the person who hurt you, your point of view is as yet slanted as a result of the molding that you've been exposed to. Practically, you can't see straight; in this manner, your "picker" for a decent mate isn't working at a high limit.

The thing is, you need uninterrupted alone time to reflect, grieve, lament, cry, rage at what has befallen you. This must be done alone because the fact of the matter is inside you, not inside another person, so that is the place you should invest your energy. What's more, would you genuinely like to hazard succumbing to another person who ends up being a similar sort of terrible news you're utilized to? No chance, not worth taking the risk. So help yourself out and keep that vehicle you're driving in its path by not being enticed to veer off and get any attractive drifters you may pass on your way.

6. Be a gray rock when it comes to your ex.

In case you're out strolling by the stream, or on a soil street, or down a rear entryway, have you at any point halted and focused on the dark rocks that may show up on the way? You haven't. A dim stone? Why in the world would somebody get one? It's merely so uninteresting, which is what you need your narcissistic ex to see you as. Otherwise, if your ex needs to take you back down (narcissists like to have a decent round of pick-ups with the exploited), or if you may be in trouble, then you may fall into a lot of wandering and imaginable Love bombarded. The front is to reject or crush you.

Narcissists blossom with dramatization and supply. They are passionate vampires whose solitary goal is to drain the life out of anybody with a thumping heart. You'll see this in your correspondence (if you have any) with them. In case you want to protect yourself from what they blame, in case you want to fight for your goal, or if you're going to open an entrance, no matter how hard they push at that point, they welcome-congratulations-you Has recently fallen into trouble and caught the trap. This is why a black stone will save your mental stability and maintain you on that street forward instead of hammering on the brakes each time your vampire ex is anxious for blood.

So don't let them see your thumping heart. Be the stone. The dark stone. Be exhausting to the point that a narcissist will lose intrigue and get other fish to get. Try not to give a narcissist what they need, which is a response — any response, regardless of if it's a negative or positive one. Narcissists couldn't care less. What they do think about is getting under your skin, pressing your catches, and actuating a passionate response that they would then be able to ridicule you for and consider a "win."

I propose finding a genuine dim stone (you'll be astounded at what number of them there are once you begin focusing) and keeping it close when and on the off chance that you need to cooperate with your ex. What's more, the honor for the best on-screen character as a dark stone goes to…

Chapter 14: Rebuild Self Esteem

When you have a short experience with a narcissist, you probably won't understand that the individual has a personality disorder exemplified by being self-consumed and lacking in compassion for other people. When you target narcissistic abuse and are involved with this individual, your consistent life gets confounding and painful.

Before you start learning, you can re-establish your self-esteem, how we can pause for a minute to describe the behavior of narcissists who may not know the meaning of the term. A person with an incredible experience of narcissistic personality problems deserves constant recognition and telling them that they are better than anyone else, smarter, and eligible for the best treatment for everyone. They complain effectively and blow up rapidly if they interpret a comment just like an insult. In their desire for attention, they can be charming when they need something from another person. Afterward, if they are denied will have a practically moment change into being extremely angry.

They rush to pass judgment on others as inferior. They appreciate utilizing phrases that are racist, demeaning, and disdainful of different groups of individuals.

For instance, a narcissist, feeling he is better than every other person, will ordinarily make statements like, "The majority are asses!"

A few people like to state that a narcissist is somebody with an abundance of self-esteem or vanity, which genuinely doesn't accomplish more than giving a surface definition. To know more, you need to comprehend how this issue started. It is ordinarily expressed in meanings the disorder that began with trauma early in childhood, during the stage when the youngster ought to have been building up a definite feeling of self. This child is usually treated harshly (including neglect) to believe that his condition is terrible. Since childhood, narcissists usually maintain an open personality, such as the pleasant Mr. Guy or Ms. Superb, because they appreciate (and need) that they can be exciting and awesome by getting along with others. Often, narcissists do favor others and expect more generous rewards. If you have been intimately involved with a narcissist, you before long found that regardless of how much consideration and to love you showered on this individual, it was rarely enough. The individual in question consistently requested an ever-increasing extent while griping that you are childish, cold, and inert. It's a hopeless scenario for you when you are right now relationship. Your confidence is pounded each day as though you are his verbal punching sack!

First, you should end or breakpoint the touch you have with this individual to mend from narcissistic maltreatment. If you are hitched or in a close connection with the narcissist, the best response for your own psychological and passionate wellbeing is to leave.

If the narcissist is a family member or somebody you work with, figure out how to restrict the time you spend in their company, and figure out how to define limits to support yourself confidently.

Presently, on to 5 hints to assist you with rebuilding your confidence and making it considerably more grounded than before you engaged with the narcissist.

1. Understand that the narcissist is a sick individual. That isn't a reason for their behavior. Yet, it is a clarification that will assist you with discharging your comments and treatment instead of holding on to the pain. Understand that although their assaults felt exceptionally personal, those comments in a narcissistic rage were the carrying on of a sick individual who has no skills for true love. Their words are not a genuine assessment or evaluation of who you are true as an individual.

2. Invest some energy throughout the following not many days or weeks writing in a diary or PC archive about violent scenes or explicit articulations he made that continue ringing a bell. Compose those down. And afterward, take a gander at them as though it was something an outsider said. As a rule, narcissists make wild allegations and little remarks intended to cut you off at the knees, causing you to feel terrible about yourself as though you are useless. However, presently what I need you to do, is take a gander at a couple of those models you've composed and asked how you would have responded if an outsider said that to you. More often than not, what you'll find is that the remark was incredible! The force they held over you was in the non-verbal communication and utilized, and in the manner in which they derided things that you held dear to your heart. This activity will assist you with discharging every one of those old damages and just let them float off on the breeze. Try not to keep on rehashing his words in your mind and once more, figuring out what he might have implied because that keeps the torment crisp as though he is as yet shoving you. What he meant was to harm

you. The words were the weapon he used to control and overwhelm you. By overcoming you, he felt all the more impressive for, in any event, a couple of seconds while you fell or responded. In that power, he had a short encounter of feeling that he was "okay" rather than the extremely sub-par individual he accepts he is nevertheless will never admit to.

3. Get going, get dynamic with work out, sports, perusing supportive books, going out with companions, learning another leisure activity, or how to cook another dish you always needed to attempt. Abstain from lounging around feeling frustrated about yourself and thinking about what's going on with you. In all probability, the narcissist picked you as their objective since you have such vast numbers of superb characteristics they are missing and envy you for having. You are likely an extraordinarily kind-hearted and caring individual, and the abuser played off that liberal soul of yours, realizing they could rely on you to remain and pardon their conduct over and over.

4. It is safe to say that you are as yet relaxing? A relationship with a narcissistic abuser can feel wrecking. However, notice that you are still alive, which implies there is more for you to do and appreciate right now, from misuse. Some portion of your inheritance is that you have the right to enjoy an actual existence that you genuinely love. You cause your fantasies to materialize and feel more joyful than you at any point, accepted conceivable. You can accomplish this change from casualty to triumphant by declining to allow the abuser to win. Excuse every one of those negative things the person in question attacked you with.

5 Consistently resend the confirmation message to yourself several times so that anyone can hear it. If you can imagine, then you will listen to a voice revealing the following to you: "I did the necessary thing, I Enough, I am enough." Use the strength of the positive testimonials to build a high degree of confidence to continually replace the old negative expressions that you admit to being obvious because abusers often speak them so frequently with extraordinary power. It is not an overnight process to rebuild your self-esteem when you have been over and again mishandled by an accomplice or parent with a personality disorder. However, don't surrender. Maintain your attention on building a life for yourself where you only attract loving individuals and loving events to you, and you will soon smiling and enjoying peace of mind and glowing, healthy self-esteem

Recovery from Narcissistic Abuse - To Get Your Life Back On Track

Narcissism or Narcissistic Personality Disorder (NPD) is a psychological issue that includes a persevering example of gaudiness. The individual with this issue continually needs to be appreciated, is fixated, and charmed by himself. The narcissistic individual additionally needs sympathy and compassion; she is heartless, self-important, looking for predominance and satisfaction. To manage and live with a narcissistic can leave somebody too damaged because of the psychological mistreatment, the narcissistic accomplice has caused. You may find that it is hard to escape from that relationship on the off chance that you were hitched to a narcissist. If you make a getaway, your recovery will be long and excruciating. Regardless of how troublesome the way to recovery is, you need to overcome it with the goal that your life will be in the groove again.

• You need to realize what the characteristics of a narcissistic individual are. It would incorporate a regular showcase of desire, treachery, control, lying, instability, verbal, and even physical maltreatment. If these practices are not pardoned and are regularly endured, it would appear to the narcissistic individual that they are worthy. On the off chance that you were effective in leaving a narcissistic accomplice or life partner, he will bait you back once more. As much as you love this individual, you must be firm in telling him that his narcissistic conduct may just be settled with the assistance of an expert. He should look for proficient help to address his damaging character, or he won't change. Being controlled and accepting that your ex will change voluntarily will just take you back to a hopeless and excruciating life.

• In recouping, you likewise need to understand that you are your total individual. At the point when you chose to be seeing someone wed a narcissistic individual, you may have just evolved reliance on that individual. He may have caught your heart with his mindful, liberal, and smooth character. This, at that point, came about to your enthusiastic reliance on him that, in the end, turned out as something for you to lament. Once you got away from the coupling relationship with a narcissist, put forth a valiant effort to recover your enthusiastic freedom. It will assist you with being firm and ready to stand again all alone. Figure out how to cherish and acknowledge your self-esteem. Set your gauges for whoever will before long come into your life. Try not to recognize anybody whose traits are not precisely the benchmarks you have selected. You realize you legitimately merit.

• Different materials are presently accessible online about managing narcissism. These assets will help you in seeing increasingly about this issue. Your picked up information will enable you to acknowledge what shortcomings have made you caught in the narcissistic trap.

• You may likewise search for gatherings and associations where you can be a piece of. These gatherings offer assistance and a chance to impart and interface with others who have endured and persevered through narcissistic connections. These are the individuals with whom you should be with. Together you can rouse each other and help each other get total recuperation and opportunity from your experience.

Chapter 15: Mistakes In Dealing With Abuse

When you forget an abuser's motives, you may naturally react in some of these ineffective ways:

1. Pacification. If you appease to maintain a strategic distance from struggle and outrage, it enables the abuser, who considers it a shortcoming and a chance to apply more control.

2. Arguing. This additionally shows shortcomings, which narcissists detest in themselves as well as other people. They may respond contemptuously with hatred or nauseate.

3. Withdrawal. This is a decent transitory strategy to gather your considerations and feelings; however, it isn't a viable procedure to manage misuse.

4. Contending and Fighting. Contending over the realities squanders your vitality. Most abusers aren't keen on the realities, yet just in advocating their position and being correct. Verbal contentions can rapidly rise to battles that channel and harm you. Nothing is picked up. You lose and can wind up feeling misled, hurt, and sad.

5. Clarifying and Defending. Anything past a just disavowal of a fraudulent incrimination leaves you open to more maltreatment. At the point when you address the substance of what is being said and clarify and shield your position, you underwrite an abuser's entitlement to pass judgment, favor, or misuse you. Your response sends this message: "You have control over my confidence. You reserve the option to affirm or object to me. You're qualified to be my adjudicator."

6. Looking for Understanding. This can drive your conduct on the off chance that you frantically need to be comprehended.

It depends on the bogus expectation that a narcissist is keen on getting you. In contrast, a narcissist is just keen on winning contention and having a prevalent position. Contingent on the level of narcissism, sharing your sentiments may likewise open you to progressively damage or control. It's smarter to impart your sentiments to somebody safe who thinks about them.

7. Censuring and Complaining. Although they may act intensely because abusers are essentially uncertain, inside, they're delicate. They can dish it, however, can't take it. Griping or reprimanding an abuser can incite fierceness and malice.

8. Dangers. Causing dangers too can prompt reprisal or blowback on the off chance that you don't do them. Never take a risk you're not prepared to uphold. Limits with direct results are progressively successful.

9. Disavowal. Try not to fall into the snare of renunciation by pardoning, limiting, or supporting maltreatment. Furthermore, don't fantasize that it will leave or improve later on. The more it goes on, the more it develops, and the more fragile you can turn into.

10. Self-Blame. Do not reprimand yourself for an abuser's activities and invest more energy to be great. This is fancy. You can't make anybody misuse you. You're just answerable for your conduct. You will never be ideal enough for an abuser to stop their behavior, which originates from their instabilities, not you.

Chapter 16: Treatment Modalities And Therapies

TREATMENT What are Effective Therapist Based Treatments? We are aware of no strong treatment results outcomes on NPD. It is hard to find a large sample of people with NPD who need to be treated. If you think you are superior to others, have high confidence, and are glad, for what reason would you look for psychotherapy?

There is surely a small percentage of individuals with NPD who do have some knowledge about their problem and would like to change, yet this isn't the standard. The lack of treatment outcome research for NPD is a significant issue that should be tended to. Despite the absence of treatment result research on NPD, there is a wealth of clinical treatment reports. These reports share two normal similitudes: (1) narcissism is hard to treat. The medicines are not regularly compelling, and (2) one key in treatment is to frame a solid union with the client. This union is urgent to urging the customer to stay in treatment. Beyond these basics, there are three overall helpful methodologies: a psychodynamic approach, a relational method, and an intellectual conduct approach, each extensively characterized (Millon, 1999).

The verifiably most established of the methodologies is psychodynamic. These medications depend to a great extent on crafted by Kernberg (1975) and Kohut (1977). The two had comparable perspectives on the presence of narcissism. Yet, they contrasted as far as etiology, with Kernberg looking toward youth abandonment issues as a source, and Kohut underlining an absence of reflecting in adolescence. More recently, specialists, for example, James Masterson, have concentrated their practices on personality disorder. These endeavors have delivered elegantly composed records both of treatment and the NARCISSISTIC PERSONALITY DISORDER 427 confusion (e.g., Masterson, 1988; 1999). The shared trait in these methodologies is that they center on negative youth experience as crucial to NPD's etiology. They also utilize excellent powerful treatment (e.g., analysis of transference and countertransference, interpretation). It is also imperative to note that this perspective on narcissism's etiology contrasts uniquely from the learning model of narcissism proposed by Millon (e.g., Millon and Davis, 1996). Millon theorizes that narcissism is found out from guardians who overestimate their offspring. Relational methodologies are gotten from the convention of Sullivan. Relational methods center on the structure of social relationships, at various times, in treatment. Specifically, the individual's representations of those relationships are investigated. The relational methodology has given some promise in treating disorders, such as NPD with solid interpersonal components (Benjamin, 1993). (We ought to likewise take note that group treatment isn't by and large prescribed for NPD [Millon, 1999]). Later intellectual, social methodologies center around the present appearances of narcissism and the insights that go with them. These are grandiose self-views, lack of empathy, and reactance to negative feedback.

The objective of the treatment is to direct these convictions. Such techniques can extend from the carefully subjective (e.g., Beck and Freeman, 1990) to others that remember a concentration for the past progressively commonplace of psychodynamic treatments. For instance, pattern treatment (Young, Klosko, and Weishar, 2003) centers around improving early subjective compositions or mental portrayal of self and others. As noticed, these various ways to deal with treatment have been utilized successfully with NPD. Yet, there is no huge scope treatment result examines. Given this absence of information, two other treatment approaches merit thought.

There is a potential treatment for NPD that includes strengthening the narcissism instead of limiting it. For instance, this methodology might be worthwhile in older populaces (Jacobowitz and Newton, 1999). Strengthening the customer's narcissism should expel certain indications, particularly those including discouragement. Second, a few treatment types depend on the conventional reflection system of "care" utilized for a scope of mental issues (e.g., Baer, 2003; Roemer and Orsillo, 2002). Of specific note, care methods have been utilized adequately as a major aspect of a more extensive rationalistic conduct treatment (DBT) for people with marginal character issues (Linehan, 1993). Care practice has been utilized in the East for centuries to battle conceit. It is conceivable that these strategies may well demonstrate helpful in limiting narcissism. What are Effective Self-Help Treatments?

There are no known successful self-improvement medications for NPD. There are numerous discussion groups on NPD; however, these are principally focused on the individuals who have been exploited by narcissists, not on the narcissists themselves.

Narcissism establishes the whole character. It is all-unavoidable. Being a narcissist is similar to being a drunkard, however considerably more so. Liquor abuse is indiscreet conduct. Narcissists show many correspondingly careless practices, some of the wild (like their wrath, the result of their injured pretentiousness). Narcissism isn't an occupation. Narcissism looks like gloom or a different issue and can't be changed freely.

Grown-up obsessive narcissism is not any more "reparable" than the total of one's character is dispensable. The patient is a narcissist. Narcissism is progressively much the same as the shade of one's skin instead of one's selection of subjects at the college.

Additionally, the Narcissistic Personality Disorder (NPD) is much of the time determined to have other, significantly progressively recalcitrant character issue, psychological instabilities, and substance misuse.

Psychological Behavioral Therapies (CBTs)

CBT accepts such knowledge-whether it is simple oral or academic knowledge-enough to trigger enthusiastic results. Suppose it is properly controlled, verbal symbols, knowledge points, and standard sentence surveys. In that case, we can say ("I am shocked", "I am worried that no one wants to be with me"), internal discussions and stories, and reshaping The standard of silence for individual behavior (learning practice) combined with constructive (and rarely pessimistic) fortifications-enough to trigger an overall enthusiastic impact commensurate with the repair. Psychodynamic hypotheses don't accept that discernment can impact feelings. They accept that many further strata must be gotten to and concentrated by both patient and specialist. The very presence of these strata is viewed as adequate to actuate a dynamic of recuperating. The specialist's job is to decipher the material uncovered to the patient (therapy) by permitting the patient to move past understanding and superimpose it on the advisor - or to effectively take part in giving a safe enthusiastic holding condition helpful for changes in the patient.

The tragic actuality is that no realized treatment is viable with narcissism ITSELF - however, a couple of treatments are sensibly fruitful to the extent adapting to a portion of its belongings goes (conduct adjustment).

Dynamic Psychotherapy Or then again Psychodynamic Therapy, Psychoanalytic Psychotherapy
Instead of regular feelings, it isn't analysis. It is an escalated psychotherapy BASED on the psychoanalytic speculation WITHOUT the (significant) segment of free association. It isn't the situation that free alliance isn't used - simply that it's not a mainstay of the system in unique treatments. Dynamic treatments are generally applied to patients not considered "reasonable" for analysis (for example, Personality Disorders, except for the Avoidant PD).

Commonly, various methods of understanding are utilized and different strategies acquired from different medicines modalities. Yet, the material deciphered isn't the aftereffect of free affiliation or dreams. The psychotherapist is significantly more dynamic than the psychoanalyst.

These medicines are open-finished. At the beginning of the treatment, the advisor (examiner) settles on an understanding (an "agreement") with the analyst and (customer or patient). The settlement says that the patient grasps to research his issues, paying little mind to what degree it takes (and how outrageous it becomes). This will gradually release the help conditions. The patient realizes that the specialist can serve him/her at any time, no matter how many meetings are needed to introduce a difficult topic.

Here and there, these treatments are partitioned to expressive versus steady; however, I view this division as misdirecting.

Expressive techniques are uncovering (=making aware) the patient's conflicts and thinking about his/her barriers and protections. The investigator deciphers the contention taking into account the new information, and directed the treatment towards the contention goals. The contention is "deciphered away" through knowledge and the patient's adjustment inspired by his/her bits of knowledge.

The strong treatments look to fortify the Ego. They explain that a strong Ego can adjust better (and later on, alone) with outside (situational) inner (impulses, drives) pressures. Steady treatments look to expand the patient's capacity to REPRESS conflicts

Group Therapies

Narcissists are notoriously unacceptable for community-oriented endeavors of any sort, not to mention group treatment. They immediately size up others as probable Sources of Narcissistic Supply. They admire the principal (providers) and devalue the latter (competitors). This isn't helpful for group therapy.

Also, the dynamic of the group will undoubtedly reflect the interactions of its individuals. Narcissists are individualists. They respect alliances with scorn and disdain. The need to cooperate, adhere to group rules, capitulate to an arbitrator, and respect and regard different individuals as equivalents - is seen by them to be humiliating and degrading (a contemptible weakness). Therefore, a gathering containing at least one narcissist is probably going to vary between present moment, exceptionally little size, coalitions (based on "superiority" and disdain), and outbreaks (acting outs) of rage and pressure.

Conclusion

Grown-up narcissists can rarely be "cured"; however, a few researchers think otherwise. The earlier the therapeutic intercession, the better the diagnosis. The right diagnosis and an appropriate mix of treatment modalities in adolescents ensure success without backsliding in anyplace between 33% and one-half of the cases. Also, maturing enhances or even vanquishes some antisocial behaviors.

In their fundamental tome, "Personality Disorders in Modern Life" (New York, John Wiley, and Sons, 2000), Theodore Millon and Roger Davis compose: "Most narcissists strongly oppose psychotherapy. A few entanglements are hard to maintain a strategic distance from for the individuals who decide to stay in treatment. Understanding and even general appraisal are regularly hard to achieve..." The 3rd edition of the "Oxford Textbook of Psychiatry" cautions: Individuals can't change their propensities, but can simply change their conditions. There has been some progress in finding strategies for influencing little changes in character; however, the management still comprises a great extent of helping the individual discover a lifestyle that conflicts less with his name.

The reason narcissism is under-reported and healing over-stated is that smart narcissists are fooling therapists. Most narcissists are expert manipulators, and they learn how to deceive their therapists.

Here are some hard facts:

There are degrees and shades of narcissism. The contrast between two narcissists can be extraordinary. The presence of affectedness and compassion or scarcity in that department are not minor varieties. They are not kidding indicators of future elements. The visualization is vastly improved on the off chance that they do exist. There are spontaneously healing cases and "short-term NPD" [see Gunderson's and Roningstam's work, 1996]. The prognosis for a classical NPD case (gaudiness, absence of compassion and all) is positively not acceptable to the extent long-term, enduring, and complete recuperating. Also, narcissists are strongly disliked by therapists.

BUT...

Side effects, co-morbid disorders (for example, Obsessive-Compulsive behaviors) and a few parts of NPD (the dysphorias, the paranoiac measurements, the results of the sense of entitlement, the neurotic lying) can be adjusted (utilizing talk treatment and, contingent upon the issue, prescription). These are not a present moment or complete solutions - yet some do have long term impacts.

The DSM is a billing and administration oriented diagnostic tool. It is planned to "tidy" up the therapist's work desk. Personality Disorders are not well divided. The differential analyses are dubiously characterized. There are some social predispositions and decisions [see the indicative criteria of the Schizotypal PD]. The outcome is sizeable disarray and numerous findings ("co-dismalness"). NPD was introduced to the DSM in 1980 [DSM-III]. There isn't sufficient research to validate any view or speculation about NPD. Future DSM releases may abrogate it through and through inside the system of a group or a solitary "character issue" class. The difference between HPD, BPD, ASPD, and NPD is my psyche, somewhat obscured. At the point when we ask: "Can NPD be healed?" we have to understand that we don't know without a doubt what is NPD and what comprises long term healing in the case of an NPD. Some individuals truly guarantee that NPD is a social disease with a cultural determinant.

Narcissists in Therapy
In treatment, the idea is to make the conditions for the True Self to proceed with its improvement: prosperity, consistency, love, equity, and acknowledgment - a holding and reflecting condition. Treatment should give these conditions of nurturance and the direction critical to achieving these goals (psychological remarking or various techniques). The narcissist must realize that his past experiences are not laws of nature. Not all adults are oppressive; that relationship can be sustaining and strong.

A lot of therapists try to co-opt the narcissist's inflated ego and defenses. They supplement the narcissist, provoking him to demonstrate his transcendence overcoming his disorder. They offer to his journey for flawlessness, splendor, and unceasing adoration - and his neurotic inclinations - trying to dispose of counterproductive, foolish, and dysfunctional behavior patterns.

By stroking the narcissist's grandiosity, they would like to adjust errors, counter subjective shortages, and the narcissist's victim-stance. They contact the narcissist to alter his behavior. Some people will experience the degree of medical treatment of the problem. They will attribute it to genetic or biochemical roots, then "free" the narcissist from guilt and obligation, and focus his spiritual resources on treatment. Going up against the narcissist head-on and taking part in power legislative issues ("I am cleverer," "My will ought to win, etc.) is firmly unhelpful and could prompt anger assaults and a developing of the narcissist's persecutory fancies, reared by his mortification in the restorative setting.

Successes have been accounted for by applying 12-advance procedures (as modified for patients experiencing the Antisocial Personality Disorder), and with treatment modalities as differing as EMDR (Eye Movement Desensitization), and NLP (Neurolinguistic Programming), Schema Therapy.

However, whatever the kind of talk therapy, the narcissist undervalues the therapist. His internal conversation is: " I know everything, I know best, the therapist is less intelligent than I, I can't bear the cost of the top-level therapists who are the main ones qualified to treat me (as my equivalents, obviously), I am an advisor myself..."

A reiteration of self-daydream and fabulous pretentiousness (truly, protections and protections): "He (my therapist) ought to be my colleague, in specific regards it is he who ought to acknowledge my professional authority, is there any valid reason why he won't be my companion, after everything I can utilize the dialect (psycho-jibber jabber) surprisingly better than he does? It's us (him and me) against an antagonistic and oblivious world (Habits a-Deux)..."

Then, there is: "Who exactly does he think he is, asking me all these questions? What are his professional credentials? I am a success, and he is no one important advisor in a shabby office, he is attempting to nullify my uniqueness, he is a power figure, I hate him, I will show him, I will mortify him, demonstrate him uninformed, have his permit renounced (transference). He is pitiable, a zero, a failure..."

Furthermore, this is just in the initial three meetings of the therapy. This injurious inside exchange turns out to be increasingly cruel and disparaging as treatment advances.

Narcissists are opposed to receiving medication. Falling back on medications is a suggested confirmation that something isn't right. Narcissists are control freaks. Additionally, many of them accept that medication is the "great equalizer" - it will cause them to lose their uniqueness, prevalence, etc. That is except if they can convincingly introduce the demonstration of accepting their meds as "heroism," a piece of a challenging venture of self-investigation, a distinctive component, etc.

They frequently claim that the medication influences them uniquely than it does to others. They have found a new, energizing method for utilizing it, or that they are a part of somebody's (normally themselves) learning curve. Narcissists must sensationalize their lives to feel special and worthy, the most uncommon. Aut nihil aut unique - either be special or not. Narcissists are drama queens.

9 789564 023632